D0056512

The

Bichon Frise

An Owner's Guide To

A HAPPY HEALTHY PET

Howell Book House

Hungry Minds, Inc.

Best-Selling Books • Digital Downloads • e-Books • Answer Networks

e-Newsletters • Branded Web Sites • e-Learning

New York, NY • Cleveland, OH • Indianapolis, IN

Howell Book House
Hungry Minds, Inc.
909 Third Avenue
New York, NY 10022
www.hungryminds.com

For general information on Hungry Minds books in the U.S., please call our Consumer Customer Service department at 800-762-2974. In Canada, please call (800) 667-1115. For reseller information, including discounts and premium sales, please call our Reseller Customer Service department at 800-434-3422.

Library of Congress Cataloging-in-Publication Data

Vogel, Mary and Kathie D.
The bichon frise: an owner's guide to happy, healthy pet/by Mary Vogel, Kathie D. Vogel.
p.cm.
Includes bibliographical references
ISBN 0-87605-480-7
I. Bichon frise(Dogs)as pets. I. Title. II. Series.
SF429.B52V64 1996, 2001
636.7'2—dc20 96-10842
CIP

Manufactured in the United States of America
10 9 8

Series Director: Kira Sexton
Book Design: Michele Laseau
Cover Design: Michael Freeland
Photography Editor: Richard Fox
Illustration: Jeff Yesh
Photography:
Front and back cover photos supplied by Winter/Churchill/DOGPHOTO.COM
Joan Balzarini: 96
Mary Bloom: 38, 96, 136, 145
Paulette Braun/Pets by Paulette: 8, 12, 14, 22, 23, 27, 62, 70, 78
Buckinghamhill American Cocker Spaniels: 148
Sian Cox: 134
Dr. Ian Dunbar: 98, 101, 103, 111, 116–17, 122, 123, 127
Rolande Lloyd: 16, 24
Dan Lyons: 96
Cathy Merrithew: 129
Outdoor Life Photography: 5
Liz Palika: 133
Janice Raines: 132
Judith Strom: 15, 33, 40, 47, 96, 107, 110, 128, 130, 135, 137, 139, 140, 144, 149, 150
Shel Styles: 2–3, 28, 30, 39, 45, 56, 58, 69, 72
Mary Vogel: 26, 61
Jean Wentworth: 33, 36–37, 40, 42, 47
Kerrin Winter & Dale Churchill: 96–97
A Bichon, by Henriette Ronner-Knip (page 21), used with permission of Lois Morrow

Contents

Welcome

to the

World

of the

part one 

Bichon Frise

External Features of the Bichon Frise

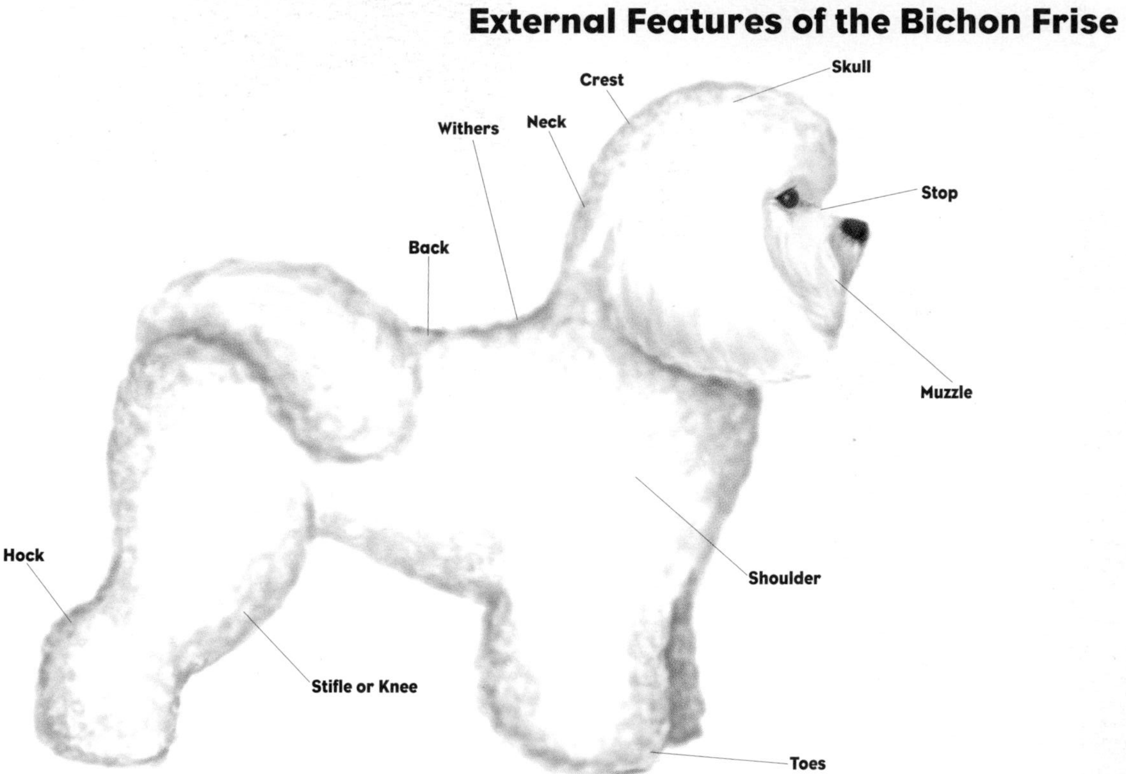

chapter 1

What Is a Bichon Frise?

This remarkable little breed has been described in many ways by many people. Bichons have various traits that make them desirable house pets; they are quite adaptable and can fit most lifestyles. When Bichon owners are asked why they admire the breed, the answers are numerous.

They are intelligent.

They're family oriented and love children.

They do well with other animals.

They're merry.

They smile.

They don't shed or have a "doggy odor."

They're terrific show dogs.

Their size is great—not too large and certainly not tiny.

They are sturdy and long living.

They are cute!!

(For a further discussion of the personality and temperament of the Bichon, see Chapter 3, "The World According to the Bichon Frise.")

Clearly, there are as many different reasons to own a Bichon as there are people who own them. However, there are important and fundamental similarities too. The reason you chose a purebred dog was because you already had an idea about what you could expect from the dog's personality, size, looks and build. Because breeders are careful to maintain a breed's distinct characteristics, one Bichon looks similar to another, and has a similar temperament. So, how do breeders know how to keep breeding Bichons that look and act like Bichons?

AKC Standards

Each American Kennel Club (AKC)–registered or AKC-recognized breed has an official standard—a guideline to present breeders with a blueprint of the dog. Every AKC breed has its own unique standard; without one how would breeders know whether they were breeding the proper and necessary traits to keep each breed unique and separate?

The American Kennel Club's standards include both a written standard and an illustrated standard. Most breeds have a tape available for the general public from the AKC. The Bichon Frise has one, and it is quite nice. If you are lucky your local library will have one available to you, and we highly recommend that you view this—particularly if there are not many Bichons in your area. This will prcsent you with a gauge by which you can judge the quality of the Bichons when you start searching for one. After all, not only is the temperament important to you, but you want your Bichon to look like a Bichon!

In the standard, the major parts of the dog are listed and discussed in sufficient detail so that when they are visualized in their proper perspective one has a complete picture of the dog described. It is of the utmost importance that the standard be understood if one is to profess that he or she is a knowledgeable breeder or conformation judge (conformation refers to the structure of the body). Breeders and conformation judges must be able to readily recognize a dog of their breed and whether it is a quality dog or not.

THE AMERICAN KENNEL CLUB

Familiarly referred to as "the AKC," the American Kennel Club is a nonprofit organization devoted to the advancement of purebred dogs. The AKC maintains a registry of recognized breeds and adopts and enforces rules for dog events including shows, obedience trials, field trials, hunting tests, lure coursing, herding, earthdog trials, agility and the Canine Good Citizen program. It is a club of clubs, established in 1884 and composed, today, of over 500 autonomous dog clubs throughout the United States. Each club is represented by a delegate; the delegates make up the legislative body of the AKC, voting on rules and electing directors. The American Kennel Club maintains the Stud Book, the record of every dog ever registered with the AKC, and publishes a variety of materials on purebred dogs, including a monthly magazine, books and numerous educational pamphlets. For more information, contact the AKC at the address listed in Chapter 13, "Resources," and look for the names of their publications in Chapter 12, "Recommended Reading."

A Quality Dog

What is meant by a quality dog? Quality can be defined in many ways. The answer may be simplified by saying the dog conforms closely to the befitting AKC standard. If the standard says the skull is to be broad, the muzzle short, the nose large, and the eyes round, then we start getting a visual picture of the head. If this dog's skull is narrow with a long muzzle and an almond eye, it should already be obvious that this dog does not conform to the standard.

Let's look at another dog. This one has the correct broad skull accompanied by a medium-length muzzle and a small nose. Is this then a quality dog? Perhaps it is, as long as the rest of the dog conforms to its AKC

standard! Remember, there is no "perfect" dog, though we strive to breed one.

I hope these examples prove how important it is for the breeders of today to strive to adhere to the AKC standards. Ethical breeders have a great responsibility both to the breed they are involved with and to the general public. When searching for your perfect pet puppy, contact the American Kennel Club or a local all-breed club for a listing of breeders in your area, or ask for a reference from your veterinarian. Try to look at a lot of puppies before purchasing one. If the person you buy your dog from is ethical, your experience dealing with him or her will be both rewarding and educational. You will be able to see the mother of the litter, and in many cases the siblings, father and maybe even the grandparents! If so, aren't you ahead of the game? If you see that they all look similar, and all have the temperament you desire in your pet, then it only stands to reason that the dog you purchase should be the same! Most ethical breeders will have you sign a spay/neuter contract if you purchase a puppy from them. This is so you, as the novice, do not take a pet quality puppy and breed it indiscriminately.

The overall impression of a Bichon comes partially from the intense and intelligent expression of the black eyes.

Who Should Breed?

Quality breeders strive to protect their breed. If they have deemed a puppy as "pet quality," it is because that puppy has an undesirable trait that they do not want passed along to the next generation. This undesirable trait may be something as minute as a back too long, a crooked tooth or ears that sit on the head too high—things that don't matter for a pet. Leave the hard work to the breeders and you take home the results of all their fine effort and work—and enjoy a beautifully bred perfect pet!

The AKC Standard for the Bichon Frise

Bichons keep looking like Bichons because breeders breed according to the AKC standard, so let's talk standard. In the following discussion, the official AKC standard appears in italics, and the authors' commentary follows.

WHAT IS A BREED STANDARD?

A breed standard—a detailed description of an individual breed—is meant to portray the *ideal* specimen of that breed. This includes ideal structure, temperament, gait, type—all aspects of the dog. Because the standard describes an ideal specimen, it isn't based on any particular dog. It is a concept against which judges compare actual dogs and breeders strive to produce dogs. At a dog show, the dog that wins is the one that comes closest, in the judge's opinion, to the standard for its breed. Breed standards are written by the breed parent clubs, the national organizations formed to oversee the well-being of the breed. They are voted on and approved by the members of the parent clubs.

General Appearance—*The Bichon Frise is a small, sturdy, white powder puff of a dog whose merry temperament is evidenced by his plumed tail carried jauntily over the back and his dark-eyed inquisitive expression.*

This is a breed that has no gross or incapacitating exaggerations and therefore there is no inherent reason for lack of balance or unsound movement.

Any deviation from the ideal described in the standard should be penalized to the extent of the deviation. Structural faults common to all breeds are as undesirable in the Bichon Frise as in any other breed, even though such faults may not be specifically mentioned in the standard.

The first impression one should have upon viewing a Bichon is that of a white powder-puff with dark impressive eyes. Dark pigment surrounding the eye is called the halo (looks like smoky eyeshadow), and this

intensifies the breed's merry expression. The black eyeliner on the entire rim of the Bichon's eye is referred to as the eye rim and is also essential—for without it the dog lacks proper expression and loses its look of keen intelligence and mischief. It has been said that one should be reminded of a little show pony when observing the Bichon's profile, for they both stand up over their hindquarters. What a clever description!

Size, Proportion and Substance—*Size—Dogs and bitches 9½ to 11½ inches are to be given primary preference. Only where the comparative superiority of a specimen outside this range clearly justifies it should greater latitude ever extend over 12 inches or under 9 inches. The minimum limits do not apply to puppies.*

Proportion—*The body from the forwardmost point of the chest to the point of rump is ¼ longer than the height at the withers. The body from the withers to lowest point of chest represents ½ the distance from withers to ground.*

Substance—*Compact and of medium bone throughout; neither coarse nor fine.*

The 9½-inch Bichon should be proportioned the same as the 12-inch Bichon. The Standard states this breed has no gross or incapacitating exaggerations, and thus balance is essential. Exaggeration in the Standard could be referring to any aspect of the dog. It could be referring to the small-proportioned dog with a head too large, resulting in a coarse-looking dog, or it could be referring to the Bichon whose leg is too long with not enough neck sporting a head too small for the rest of the body. When looking at these specimens one can only think *pinhead!* Bichons are of medium-size bone—never slight of bone like a Toy Poodle.

Head—***Expression***—*Soft, dark-eyed, inquisitive, alert.* ***Eyes*** *are round, black or dark brown and are set in the skull to look directly forward. An overly large or bulging eye is a fault as is an almond-shaped, obliquely set eye. Halos, the black or very dark brown skin surrounding the eyes, are necessary* *as they accentuate the eye and enhance expression. The eye rims themselves must be black. Broken pigment or total absence of pigment on the eye rims produces a blank and staring expression, which is a definite fault. Eyes of any color other than black or dark brown are a very serious fault and must be severely penalized.* ***Ears*** *are drop and are covered with long, flowing hair. When extended toward the nose, the leathers reach approximately halfway the length of the muzzle. They are set slightly higher than eye level and rather forward on the skull so that when the dog is alert they frame the face. The* ***skull*** *is slightly rounded, allowing for a round and forward-looking eye. The* ***stop*** *is slightly accentuated.*

Muzzle*—A properly balanced head is three parts muzzle to five parts skull, measured from the nose to the stop and from the stop to the occiput. A line drawn between the outside corners of the eyes and to the nose will create a near equilateral triangle. There is a slight degree of chiseling under the eyes, but not so much as to result in a weak or snipy foreface. The lower jaw is strong. The nose is prominent and always black.* ***Lips*** *are black, fine, never drooping.* ***Bite*** *is scissors. A bite which is undershot or overshot should be severely penalized. A crooked or out of line tooth is permissible, however, missing teeth are to be severely faulted.*

After reviewing the standard's section on the Bichon's head, it should be very clear that their heads and expressions should not look anything like a Poodle! Remember a round black eye and a moderate length of muzzle is called for in the Bichon, whereas the standard for the Poodle requires an oval eye and a long, straight and fine (not thick) muzzle. When one is looking straight on at the face of the Bichon, his muzzle should appear rather short, almost overwhelmed by his prominent black nose and intense eyes.

As the standard states, the ears should be set slightly higher than eye level. This means the top of the ear is a little higher than eye level. However most Bichon puppies' ears seem to be set too high, and gradually drop with maturity as the skull broadens and the weight of the ear fringe helps to lower them.

Neck, Topline and Body—*The arched neck is long and carried proudly behind an erect head. It blends smoothly into the shoulders. The length of neck from occiput to withers is approximately 1/3 the distance from forechest to buttocks. The* ***topline*** *is level except for a slight, muscular arc over the loin.*

Body—*The chest is well developed and wide enough to allow free and unrestricted movement of the front legs. The lowest point of the chest extends at least to the elbow. The ribcage is moderately sprung and extends back to a short and muscular loin. The forechest is well pronounced and protrudes slightly forward of the point of shoulder. The underline has a moderate tuck-up.* ***Tail*** *is well plumed, set on level with the topline and curved gracefully over the back so that the hair of the tail rests on the back. When the tail is extended toward the head it reaches at least halfway to the withers. A low tail set, a tail carried perpendicularly to the back, or a tail which droops behind is to be severely penalized. A corkscrew tail is a very serious fault.*

This puppy has the characteristic Bichon tail, carried up and over the back.

The profile of the Bichon is a gentle flow of curves beginning at the occiput, continuing with the arched long neck that flows into the withers and the level topline. While the topline is level, there is a very slight muscular arch over the loin. The Bichon's topline is trimmed level, so one must actually feel the topline in order to recognize the presence of the slight arch over the loin. This arched muscle helps the Bichon stand the way he does—with his hindquarters (rear) extended well behind him.

If you had a Bichon standing on a table and put your hands on either side of the dog, his sides should not be flat but should feel as though they curve out from the body a bit (spring of rib).

The tail has long flowing hair that is never to be severely trimmed, only neatened up. The base of the tail should start at approximately the same level as the topline. This is called the "tail set." A low tail set (one set below the topline) is to be severely penalized, for it destroys the beautiful silhouette of the breed! The tail should be held in a long graceful curve over the back. When a Bichon is unsure of a situation or frightened he will "drop" his tail so it hangs behind him.

Forequarters—*Shoulders—The shoulder blade, upper arm and forearm are approximately equal in length. The shoulders are laid back to somewhat near a forty-five-degree angle. The upper arm extends well back so the elbow is placed directly below the withers when viewed from the side.* ***Legs*** *are of medium bone; straight with no bow or curve in the forearm or wrist. The elbows are held close to the body. The* ***pasterns*** *slope slightly from the vertical. The dewclaws may be removed. The* ***feet*** *are tight and round resembling those of a cat and point directly forward, turning neither in nor out.* ***Pads*** *are black.* ***Nails*** *are kept short.*

The medium-size bones should be straight. Under no circumstances should one forgive a bow or an exaggerated curve in the forearm or at the wrist, yet this is a breed fault that haunts breeders from time to time. When Bichons were first introduced to the United States in 1956, they had just this problem: bowed front legs that were rather short. We American breeders decided that the Bichon would be sounder if we added length to the legs and straightened the forelegs. We were absolutely correct, for today's Bichon is one of the soundest and most efficient in the canine world. Ta-da!

As in most sound movers, the Bichon requires a well-laid back shoulder, as close to a forty-five-degree angle as possible. The sternum should be prominent. This is the bone that protrudes between the point of shoulders of the forechest.

Hindquarters—*The hindquarters are of medium bone, well angulated with muscular thighs and spaced moderately*

wide. The upper and lower thigh are nearly equal in length meeting at a well bent stifle joint. The leg from hock joint to foot pad is perpendicular to the ground. Dewclaws may be removed. Paws are tight and round with black pads.

Hindquarters are medium-size bone with very muscular thighs. Due to good angulation, one can see the Bichon's black pads as the dog moves away from you.

Coat—*The texture of the coat is of utmost importance. The undercoat is soft and dense, the outercoat of a coarser and curlier texture. The combination of the two gives a soft but substantial feel to the touch which is similar to plush or velvet and when patted springs back. When bathed and brushed, the coat stands off the body, creating an overall powder puff appearance. A wiry coat is not desirable. A limp, silky coat, a coat that lies down, or a lack of undercoat are very serious faults.* ***Trimming***—*The coat is trimmed to reveal the natural outline of the body. It is rounded off from any direction and never cut so short as to create an overly trimmed or squared off appearance. The furnishings of the head, beard, mustache, ears and tail are left longer. The longer head hair is trimmed to create an overall rounded impression. The topline is trimmed to appear level. The coat is long enough to maintain the powder puff look which is characteristic of the breed.*

White, white and more white! This is the color of the Bichon Frise, though puppies may have apricot shading which they usually outgrow.

This is the icing on the cake. The coat is plush, luxurious and soft to the touch. It is soft underneath (the undercoat), yet dense with an outer coat that is curly and coarser. The combination of undercoat and outer coat enables it to "stand out" from the body, giving it that famous powder-puff look. Without the outer coat, the coat would be limp and have no body. Poor coat texture is a serious fault, for Bichons were developed for the sole purpose of being a companion dog and should be pleasing to the eye. Perhaps the coat is one of the reasons the Bichon is such a formidable competitor in all-breed shows throughout the world.

Bichons have strong and powerful movement for their size.

Another desirable characteristic of the Bichon coat is that it is nonshedding and does not carry an offensive "doggy odor." Another plus is that Bichons do not shed dander, making them more compatible to the family that has a member who is allergic.

Color—*Color is white, may have shadings of buff, cream or apricot around the ears or on the body. Any color in excess of 10 percent of the entire coat of a mature specimen is a fault and should be penalized, but color of the accepted shadings should not be faulted in puppies.*

White, white and more white! The standard does allow shadings of buff, beige, apricot and cream anywhere on the body, as long as it is no more than 10 percent. Most puppies are born with shading somewhere on their coat, the most common area being both ears. Sometimes these shadings or colored areas are very bright orange on puppies, but usually fade out or

completely disappear by the time the dog is eighteen months old. Colored areas on the Bichon should never be considered a fault unless it is over 10 percent of the entire dog. Sometimes the entire adult coat may be an off-white color, and this also is perfectly acceptable.

Gait—*Movement at a trot is free, precise and effort-less. In profile the forelegs and hind legs extend equally with an easy reach and drive that maintain a steady topline. When moving, the head and neck remain somewhat erect and as speed increases there is a very slight convergence of legs toward the center line. Moving away, the hindquarters travel with moderate width between them and the foot pads can be seen. Coming and going his movement is precise and true.*

The cheerful disposition of the Bichon makes it a perfect breed to keep with other pets.

A Bichon whose conformation (body structure) fits the AKC standard is one of the best-moving dogs there is. There is a lot of power in this sturdy, sound breed. The Bichon's structure makes it possible for a great amount of reach (lift of the front legs for ground coverage) and drive (the powerful thrust from behind that also contributes to ground coverage). The Bichon's head is held somewhat erect during movement, but as he trots faster his head and neck extend somewhat lower and out in front of him. At the faster pace his legs will slightly converge to the center line when viewed from behind; at this pace you will see the width between the hind legs close slightly. You should see the pads of the hind feet during a slow or a fast trot.

Temperament—*Gentle mannered, sensitive, playful and affectionate. A cheerful attitude is the hallmark of the breed and one should settle for nothing less.*

A cheerful attitude is a hallmark of the breed! A truer statement has never been made. These little dogs in their snowsuits will work their way into your heart and home. Once you live with a Bichon you will always have one. This is not to say that you can't have another breed, for the Bichon's gentle and nonthreatening disposition makes it possible to own other pets. In fact, he prefers another dog or cat or two! Please refer to Chapter 3 to learn more about his intelligence and temperament.

chapter 2

The Bichon Frise's Ancestry

The origin of the Bichon Frise is a bit "fuzzy," not unlike the little dog himself!

Early Origins

One school of thought is that the Bichon originated on the island of Malta, off of Spain, the product of the Maltese, Miniature Spaniel and the Miniature Poodle. Others believe the Bichon is a descendant of the Barbet, a water spaniel with a curly or "frizzy" coat from the Mediterranean.

Though the early origins are not precisely known, most Bichoners accept that the ancestors of today's Bichon arrived on the European continent in the fourteenth century with sailors who brought them to use as barter.

In Europe, four variations of the Barbet developed: the Bichon Maltese, the Bichon Bolognese, the Tenerife Bichon and the Bichon Havenese. Although these groups share a common ancestry, they are distinct breeds.

A 1944 photo of a French Bichon.

A combination of these Bichon breeds eventually formed the Bichon Frise, though we will never know in what proportions. The breed's tremendous history makes it difficult to determine the exact origins of the Bichon Frise. We do know, however, that the Bichon's ancient roots can be traced back to the era before Christ, and that at some point in its history, this breed and its predecessors have been desired by many western civilizations.

The Royal Treatment

At the time of the Renaissance in Europe, the French aristocracy acquired a fascination with Italian art and culture. Scholars, craftsmen, Italian artifacts and artists made their way to the French courts. The Bichon, too, was a fashionable trend. The little dog became a pampered pet of the royal family and those with the greatest wealth.

The king and ladies of the court carried these tiny dogs by placing them in baskets attached around their necks by colorful ribbons. It is said that King Henry III was never without the company of his Bichons. This may sound a bit too "froufrou," but remember, this was the Renaissance—the more lace, satin, bows, curls, rib-

bons and perfume, the better. In fact, the French verb "bichonner" means to pamper, to make beautiful.

Life on the Streets

At the time of the French Revolution the Bichon began to lose its favored position—as the nobility was losing theirs—and by the nineteenth century, these pampered pets were exiled to the streets to fend for themselves.

To some dogs, this would be a living end—but not so the Bichon! Because of their personalities, they made wonderful circus dogs, quick of mind, sturdy, agile, trusting and loving. There are also stories of gypsies traveling with these small dogs who could smile and perform clever tricks. As street dogs, forced to survive on their own, they quickly learned that life was much easier if you were agreeable and friendly to the world in general—a little smile could go a long way.

The Bichon's experience as a circus dog and a street performer is perfectly suited for the breed's eager-to-please disposition. Their personalities have made them perfect pets for everyone from the aristocrats of the French court, to the gypsies and street performers. (See Chapter 3 for more information on the personality and temperament of the Bichon).

Bichons still have these qualities, and I see them as a sign of intelligence. Bichons seem to "see around corners." I've been owned by them for some twenty-plus years, and I

WHERE DID DOGS COME FROM?

It can be argued that dogs were right there at man's side from the beginning of time. As soon as human beings began to document their own existence, the dog was among their drawings and inscriptions. Dogs were not just friends, they served a purpose: There were dogs to hunt birds, pull sleds, herd sheep, burrow after rats—even sit in laps! What your dog was originally bred to do influences the way it behaves. The American Kennel Club recognizes over 140 breeds, and there are hundreds more distinct breeds around the world. To make sense of the breeds, they are grouped according to their size or function. The AKC has seven groups:

1) Sporting, 2) Working,
3) Herding, 4) Hounds,
5) Terriers, 6) Toys,
7) Non-Sporting

Can you name a breed from each group? Here's some help: (1) Golden Retriever; (2) Doberman Pinscher; (3) Collie; (4) Beagle; (5) Scottish Terrier; (6) Maltese; and (7) Dalmatian. All modern domestic dogs (*Canis familiaris*) are related, however different they look, and are all descended from *Canis lupus*, the gray wolf.

still have quite a time trying to keep one step ahead of their power to think.

The Bichon in Art

It is not unusual to find a small, white, curly-coated dog in portraits done by the masters of long ago. Most of these dogs are shown with more apricot coloring than our ice-white Bichons of today. (Our current breed Standard allows apricot to be as much as 10 percent of the entire coat. See Chapter 1, "What Is a Bichon Frise?")

This painting of a Bichon by Henriette Ronner-Knip is thought to be about 100 years old.

Some of the famous portraits of Bichons were painted by Sir Joshua Reynolds (1746–1792), Francisco Goya (1746–1828) and Emile Carolus-Duran (1838–1917). This is most certainly the "proof in the pudding" as to where Bichons were and helps to substantiate their presence in different historical periods.

Usually in the old paintings the Bichon was depicted with ribbons and the feet were clean-shaven, like a trimmed Poodle foot. A painting by Henriette Ronner-Knip entitled simply "A Bichon," thought to be about

100 years old, depicts a Bichon looking very much like those of today, except for the trimmed feet. With a few grooming touches, this little fella (or girl) could be ready for the "Garden" (Westminster Kennel Club show). His head and expression are close to the desired standard of perfection.

The friendly and agreeable nature of the Bichon Frise has made it a popular pet for everyone from gypsies to kings.

The Bichon in France

In the twentieth century, there were a few dog fanciers who recognized the potential of these dogs and started to establish their own purebred lines. The dogs were known by two different names—the Tenerife Bichon and the Bichon à Poil Frise.

On March 5, 1933, the French Standard of the breed was approved by the Société Central Canine de France. It was written by Madame Bouctovagniez, president of the Toy Club of France. The name chosen was Bichon à Poil Frise (Bichon with the curly coat). If it were not for these early dedicated breeders, the Bichon Frise as we know it today would not exist.

In October 1956, Mr. and Mrs. François Picault of Dieppe, France, came to the United States with several Bichons. This was the start of it all in the United States. Breeders were obtaining dogs from the Picaults as well as actively importing dogs from France and Belgium.

FAMOUS OWNERS OF THE BICHON FRISE

Susan Lucci

Betty White

Barbara Taylor Bradford

John Forsythe

Aaron Spelling

Kathie Lee Gifford

The Bichon in the United States

The Bichon's popularity in the United States grew by leaps and bounds. They were shown in rare breed matches; local clubs were quickly being formed throughout the country. You might say that America was falling in love with the Bichon Frise! The impact was tremendous, to say the least. The Bichon Frise Club of America formed in May 1964, due to the interests and efforts of Azalea Gascoigne, Gertrude Fournier, Mayree Butler, Jean Rank and Goldie Olson.

The Bichon was pampered by royalty in Renaissance France. Today many Bichon owners treat their pets like royalty.

The Standard of the Bichon in the United States was adopted upon formation of the Bichon Frise Club of America and was approved by the American Kennel Club in November 1974. The standard was modified in 1979 and again as late as 1988. These modifications were mostly word changes to help breeders and judges better understand and interpret the meaning.

In 1972, the Bichon was officially admitted to the American Kennel Club Stud Book, which is the official record of a dog's registration with the American Kennel Club. Your dog's registration will appear in the stud book.

On September 1, 1971, the American Kennel Club permitted the Bichon Frise to compete in the Miscellaneous class at AKC dog shows. In 1973 the breed was given full recognition by the AKC and was allowed to compete for championship points and be shown in the Non-Sporting Group.

Bichon Firsts

On May 14, 1976, the first national specialty was held in San Diego, California, and was hosted by the Bichon Frise Club of San Diego. A national specialty is a show of only one breed, in this case the Bichon. It is a breeders' showcase. Best-in-Show honors went to Ch. Vogelflight's Music Man.

Through all the hard work of showing, the Bichon is a merry companion.

The first Bichon to complete his championship in the United States was Ch. C. and D. Count Kristopher. The breed's first all-breed Best in Show winner, in July 1973, was Ch. Chaminade Syncopation. The first Bichon to win Best of Breed at the Westminister Kennel Club show was Robert Koeppel's Ch. Rank's Eddie in 1974.

The Westminister Kennel Club show is held annually in mid-February and has live TV coverage. This show is considered to be the most prestigious "show of all shows"! At this show the Bichon consistently wins a placement in the Non-Sporting Group. They are beautiful and captivating show dogs, but first and above all, they are their owners' beloved companions.

After all, that is their only purpose, to be a pet and companion. And that they are.

When I think of celebrities owning Bichons, the first name that comes to mind is Betty White. The actress has been photographed numerous times with her little Bichon, said to have been rescued from an animal shelter.

chapter 3

The World According to the Bichon Frise

The Bichon thinks the world is a bowl full of cherries! These delightful little companions need only to be participating members of your family in order to be happy. Bichons are quite content to follow you throughout the day or sit by your side. However, this is not to say that they don't appreciate being the center of attention and won't perform some cute antic to be just that.

Bichons Love Company

Bichons love companionship, making them the ideal pet for the multipet household. They do well with cats and other dogs, though they seem to prefer white dogs, especially other Bichons. I have seen them shy away from large dark dogs and turn inside out over a group of dogs that are white, especially Bichons. What could provide more enjoyment than a pair of merry little Bichons greeting you at the door or snuggling up next to you while you watch your favorite TV program?

Bichons are happy, friendly dogs. "Laugh and the world will laugh with you" could be their motto.

The preferred sleeping arrangements for a Bichon is with a companion—especially a human companion. If this is not acceptable to you (and you don't know what you are missing!) a bed will need to be provided. The washable fleece-lined pet beds seem to be popular with Bichons—the fluffier the better!!

Because this breed is so playful, they make excellent companions for children. When parents ask if Bichons are good with children, I always ask, "Is the child going to be good with the Bichon?" Bichons are sturdy and healthy, but any breed needs to be supervised when playing with a small child. The Bichon may be very content being dressed up by his mistress or just as content in any adventure young master's imagination will allow. He makes the best "little pirate" and is equally content sitting quietly by grandma's side while she knits.

Though Bichons are very loving family members, they are also little traitors! Bichons are never shy and have

never met a stranger. They are usually very content staying with someone who is not a family member as long as that person dotes on them; they might even consider it being on holiday.

They also never forget a friend. Several years ago I was at a dog show talking to a friend when I heard a very demanding barking behind my back. The bark became more insistent, climaxing to a shrill scream. When I turned around there was a little Bichon waiting its turn to go into the ring. A very perplexed woman was trying to calm her down to no avail. As I approached the woman and her dog, the Bichon became ecstatic. She turned out to be a former client of mine—I had groomed and trained her as a puppy! I hadn't seen that pup for at least six months, and while I didn't recognize her at first, she certainly knew me.

Bichons make terrific playmates for children of all ages, as long as the children know how to treat them properly.

Schedules

Bichons thrive on schedules. They are most happy being fed and exercised around the same hours every day. Its not unusual to see them staring their owners down when it's feeding time, or getting antsy when its time for a walk. They are creatures of habit, and if you forget the schedule, they are intelligent enough to remind you. They can become quite clever in their methods to do so.

Bichons Need Grooming, Lots of It!

When you decide to make a Bichon part of your family, remember that they need lots of grooming attention. Their coats need brushing often to stay in top shape and keep from getting matted and dirty. They need to be bathed often to keep the white coat white, and they also need drying or their coat will curl up and look more like a Poodle's than a Bichon's. Keep in mind as you bring a Bichon into your life that this is one area that will cost you time and money. It's worth it, of course, because your Bichon will be so beautiful! (See Chapter 6, "Grooming Your Bichon Frise," for complete information on grooming your Bichon.)

> **A DOG'S SENSES**
>
> *Sight:* With their eyes located farther apart than ours, dogs can detect movement at a greater distance than we can, but they can't see as well up close. They can also see better in less light, but can't distinguish many colors.
>
> *Sound:* Dogs can hear about four times better than we can, and they can hear high-pitched sounds especially well. Their ancestors, the wolves, howled to let other wolves know where they were; our dogs do the same, but they have a wider range of vocalizations, including barks, whimpers, moans and whines.
>
> *Smell:* A dog's nose is his greatest sensory organ. His sense of smell is so great he can follow a trail that's weeks old, detect odors diluted to one-millionth the concentration we'd need to notice them, even sniff out a person under water!
>
> *Taste:* Dogs have fewer taste buds than we do, so they're likelier to try anything—and usually do, which is why it's especially important for their owners to monitor their food intake. Dogs are omnivores, which means they eat meat as well as vegetable matter like grasses and weeds.
>
> *Touch:* Dogs are social animals and love to be petted, groomed and played with.

While Bichons may be a high grooming maintenance pet, they will never put up a fight over being brushed, bathed or groomed. They love the end result, knowing that their looks please everyone, and they will show off by prancing gaily about so they can be admired. When you say "Want to go to the groomer?" your Bichon should run merrily to where his leash is kept in anticipation of his beauty-parlor day. If he does not seem to enjoy this experience, perhaps you need to look into a new groom-ing shop. Most groomers will readily share with you that, while grooming a Bichon may be a bit more time-consuming than, say, doing a Schnauzer, the Bichon is

very cooperative and patient. A day spent with the groomer should be a pleasant one, but also can be very tiring. Don't be surprised if your little angel comes home, shows off, and then promptly falls asleep for several hours!

Your Bichon is eager to please you, so be gentle in your criticisms.

The Performer

With a Bichon, you have a "performer" on your hands. A performer needs applause more than "boos." Use positive feedback, not negative scolding, as a tool in your bag of tricks. Though outgoing, this breed is also very soft-tempered and their feelings are easily hurt. You need only raise your voice to correct a Bichon—never raise your hand.

We've all heard the term "breaking a dog's spirit." What exactly does that mean? It means that most dogs want to please their owners above anything else in their world, and if they are consistently scolded they will start to react to this. The dog will urinate during a scolding or run and hide from his owner. One has to always remember that the Bichon's world is a happy one, and he'll do almost anything to keep it that way. He'll laugh with you, and most of all will make you laugh at him, so never go overboard in scolding him.

Bichons know when they look good, and they love to be praised and admired. These same traits are what make them such wonderful little show dogs. They love the preshow training and conditioning. After all, they're the center of attention. And how about all the grooming before the show? This again is "one on one" attention, and they thrive on it. And how they love being at the show! People ooh and aah and they can be around lots of other Bichons. Perfect!

Catlike

Bichons are very "catlike," loving high places such as the backs of couches and window ledges. If you don't like them in these places, you need to teach them from the time that they first enter your home that furniture is off-limits. This willing-to-please breed will easily accept these terms from the beginning, but if you let them get into the habit of sleeping on your furniture, then suddenly decide to change the rules, you're in for a challenge. Bichons think that once you've set the rules and they've learned them, that's that!

CHARACTERISTICS OF THE BICHON FRISE

Curious

Intelligent

Agile

Sweet

Comical

Loving

Healthy and long living

Athletic and Agile

The Bichon Frise was one of the original circus dogs and is very sturdy and athletic. They love learning tricks, which is accomplished most efficiently and successfully through lavish praise (treats). During training, the bond between dog and master becomes even closer and one-on-one time with your Bichon becomes fun time as well as learning time. This breed has a wonderful sense of humor and loves games such as chase and hide-and-seek.

Bichon Quirks

The Bichon has a very endearing trait known to many breeders and owners as the Bichon Buzz. Out of nowhere they will pin their ears back, tuck their tails and buzz around the room! This is usually

accompanied by a husky-sounding play-growl and hysterical laughing from their audience. This is their way of saying that all is well with them and it's great to be a Bichon!

Which reminds me—they smile! Many will actually curl their lips back, showing their teeth while squinting their eyes and wagging their entire hindquarters and fluffy tail. If one has never witnessed a canine smile it may at first be interpreted as a hostile action, but only a second later the rest of the body language shows otherwise, and both old and young can't help but smile back!

Bichons are athletic and agile and love outdoor activities.

Bichon Activities

As an AKC-recognized breed and a member of the Non-Sporting group, the Bichon Frise competes and excels in many AKC-sponsored events, among them agility and obedience.

Agility

In agility dogs race over a course of obstacles, which includes tunnels, hurdles, and planks. Many Bichons love this sport, and excel at it almost effortlessly. Agility training builds confidence in your Bichon, and strengthens the bond between you and your dog. See Chapter 9, "Getting Active with Your Dog," for more information on agility events.

Obedience

There are not a vast number of Bichons competing in the obedience ring, but they do hold their own. Because of their willingness to please, properly trained Bichons not only love the obedience ring, they are successful as well. However, be cautious when choosing a training center for your Bichon, whether you are training to learn obedience or for the sheer fun of it. The training method must be reward-based (nothing too harsh). Bichons cannot be made to feel that they have let you down—after all, that's not fun!

Therapy Dog

The Bichon Frise also excels as a therapy dog. Being close to and stroking a dog has perceptible benefits to people, including decreased blood pressure. Pets improve our lives immeasurably. However, there are those who cannot keep a pet in their lives because they live in an institutional setting such as a nursing home. Ironically, these are often the people who can benefit most from contact with a pet.

Bichons can be successful obedience competitors if they are well trained and encouraged with lots of praise.

Around the country, groups have been set up to get these people in contact with the dogs who can bring so much cheer and light into their lives. Therapy work must be done by dogs who are even-tempered, patient and good with strangers.

The special personality of the Bichon makes this breed perfect for therapy work. The Bichon is almost invariably outgoing, friendly, gentle and attractive. Their small, but not fragile, size makes them perfect for holding and cuddling. Therapy Dogs International is a good

organization to contact if you are interested in getting your Bichon involved with therapy work. See Chapter 13, "Resources," for the address of this organization.

The Bichon is an enthusiastic and adaptable breed. In addition to excelling in the above activities, this breed has proven worthy in other events, including tracking and weight pulling! Consider getting involved in an organized activity with your Bichon; your relationship and confidence will be strengthened. Just make sure you don't get too competitive with your Bichon; remember, the object of the game is always to have a good time!

MORE INFORMATION ON THE BICHON FRISE

National Breed Club

The Bichon Frise Club of America
Denise Richardson, Secretary
186 Ash Street
Twin Falls, Idaho 83301

BFCACORSEC@aol.com
www.bichon.org/bfca.htm

The club can send you information on all aspects of the breed, including the names and addresses of clubs in your area. Inquire about membership.

Books

Beauchamp, Richard. *Bichon Frises: Everything About Purchase, Care, Nutrition, Breeding, Behavior and Training.* Hauppauge, New York: Barrons Educational Series, 1996.

The Truth About Bichons. Midway City,CA: Premiere Publishing, 1998.

Dylan, Jamie. *Guide to Owning a Bichon Frise.* Neptune, New Jersey: TFH Publications, 1997.

Palika, Liz. *How to Train Your Bichon Frise.* Neptune, New Jersey: TFH Publications, 2000.

MAGAZINES

Bichon Frise Reporter
(Quarterly)
P.O. Box 6369, Dept. WEB
San Luis Obispo, CA 93412
Web: www.fix.net/~dogmag/bichon/bichon-home.html
E-mail: dogmag@fix.net
Phone (805) 528-2007
Fax (805) 528-8200

VIDEO

AMP Guide to Grooming the Bichon Frise
Order from:
4-M Enterprises, Inc.
Everything in Dog Books
34937 Pico Street
Union City, CA 94550
(800) 487-9867
Approximately 60 minutes/$48.00

WEBSITES

FAQ: The Bichon Frise
www.bichonfrise.org/faq.html

Stop by this Web site for answers to your most frequently asked Bichon questions. You will find a variety of information here everything from housetraining and grooming to personality and health.

Bichon ResQ
www.bichonrescue.org

If you're ready to adopt a pet or want to volunteer your time and energy to Bichon rescue, this is a wonderful place to start.

Bichon Frise Boutique
www.halcyon.com/dianec/sculptures/bichon.html

If you're looking for that perfect, little Bichon statuette, windsock or set of note cards, look no further.

Living

with a

part two 

Bichon Frise

chapter 4

Bringing Your Bichon Frise Home

When searching for the perfect Bichon for your family, be sure to contact many breeders and see as many adult Bichons as possible. The breeder will usually ask which sex you prefer. Most breeders will agree that the male Bichon is a little sweeter and less willful than his female counterpart. For those in search of a pet-quality Bichon, the good news is that it's usually easier to purchase a pet male than a female. Breeders can only keep a certain number of puppies from a litter, and most breeders have more females than males.

When looking at prospective Bichon puppies, study the temperament of the mother as well as the siblings. This breed is never to snap or growl at visitors. The mother may be protective of her puppies, but never of her owners, once you have been properly introduced. The puppies should be interacting with one another. If the puppies are old enough (at least eight weeks), they should be interacting with people as well. Bichons are not shy—don't settle for a poor temperament because you feel sorry for the puppy. After all, Bichons are long-lived, and you choose this little companion dog because of his merry ways!

Bringing Your New Puppy Home

We have always allowed our puppies to remain with their mothers as long as mom says its all right. Both are happier this way. There is no magic age at which a puppy should be allowed to leave its mother and go to a new home. Some puppies are secure and outgoing, while others are more dependent and want to be with their mothers. Puppies who are weaned by their mother (not the breeder) are secure throughout their lives. Interaction with mother and littermates teaches them numerous lessons. For these reasons, we feel it is not advisable to take your puppy home before ten weeks of age. By this age the puppy has already learned to enjoy his bath and has been taught to be still and stand to be brushed and scissor-trimmed. The early training is invaluable to you, your veterinarian and your dog groomer.

Give your new puppy lots of affection, but also make sure she has time to rest and adjust to her new home.

After you take the puppy home, let the newcomer meet the family, but hold off the neighbors and your children's friends until the puppy has had a few days to become accustomed to his new home. Your puppy will become tired from all the excitement and change, so expect him to explore briefly and then sleep.

He may tend to drink too much water at once. This could cause a minor stomach upset and he may throw up. Let him have his drink, but observe how much water he is drinking. If it seems to be a nervous reaction, take the water from him for a short period of time. Usually on the first night in their new homes, puppies do not care to eat.

Puppies must be handled with gentle care.

Explain to your children that young puppies are babies and should be held gently and cuddled, but not played with—they are babies, not toys. Do not allow children to pick up a puppy unless supervised. If the puppy wiggles, the child loses his hold and the puppy falls to the floor, death or permanent damage can result. When older, Bichons will be delighted to play games with the children and a long-lasting bond will develop between them.

A number of decisions, arrangements and purchases should be made prior to bringing your puppy home, including choosing a veterinarian, picking your puppy's name, pet-proofing your home, and making sure you have the necessary supplies.

Choosing a Veterinarian

One of the first things you should do after taking your new puppy home is make an appointment with your veterinarian for his first checkup. I should add, his first check-up with you. Hopefully, you bought your Bichon from a reliable source, and if so, the puppy was examined by a veterinarian and appropriate immunizations (shots) were given. If you are uncertain as to the choice of veterinarian, it would be advisable to discuss this with your puppy's breeder.

If your breeder is not in the area, ask friends and neighbors to recommend a vet. The veterinarian will give your puppy a thorough examination and check for intestinal parasites, and will also make plans for providing additional shots that are needed in the future.

Choosing a Name

Hopefully you have already chosen a name for your puppy. If not, do not wait too long, and please, do not change the name daily—this will only confuse the puppy. Make it a practice to use his name whenever you greet him or upon touching him. Use his name upon giving a command and avoid using various nicknames. Look him in the eye and talk to him in a calm, cheerful voice, and he will soon respond to your desires.

Puppy-Proofing Your Home

Always keep in mind that puppies are like toddlers. They are very inquisitive and have a desire to explore, so we must protect them and also protect our household belongings from sharp teeth. Encourage family members to keep shoes, clothing, books and papers picked up and put away where the puppy cannot reach them.

Laundry detergent, bleach, cleaning fluid, mothballs, disinfectants, fertilizer and antifreeze are some of the poisons that can be deadly. Many houseplants such as English ivy, philodendrons, caladium, poinsettias and lilies are a hazard if ingested. Last, but not least, chocolate in any form can be deadly to a dog!

HOUSEHOLD DANGERS

Curious puppies and inquisitive dogs get into trouble not because they are bad, but simply because they want to investigate the world around them. It's our job to protect our dogs from harmful substances, like the following:

IN THE HOUSE

cleaners, especially pine oil

perfumes, colognes, aftershaves

medications, vitamins

office and craft supplies

electric cords

chicken or turkey bones

chocolate

some house and garden plants, like ivy, oleander and poinsettia

IN THE GARAGE

antifreeze

garden supplies, like snail and slug bait, pesticides, fertilizers, mouse and rat poisons

Keep the candy dish out of reach and stress to your children the importance of keeping chocolate from your puppy. Puppies do not need candy! This holds true for grown dogs as well.

Make certain all lamp and other electrical cords are tied up and out of reach. If the puppy is to be left in a room unattended, it is best to place trash cans up and out of reach.

Train yourself and family members to be aware of any small objects on the floor such as tiny pieces of toys, staples, pins, etc., and just as with small children, do not allow him access to plastic bags or balloons which could suffocate him or that he could swallow. All bones from your table scraps are a big no-no. Never, never give your puppy or grown dog any bones. They can be disastrous.

If you introduce the leash in the proper way, your puppy will enjoy walking on it.

Supplies

Food and water bowls should be tip-proof, unbreakable and chew-proof. Stainless steel or heavy ceramic dishes are best and are dishwasher-safe. We like to have matching food and water bowls so they can be placed neatly side by side.

If your puppy has a tendency to play with his water bowl, take up the bowl and offer him water several times throughout the day, or use a plastic water bottle in the house and the water bowl in his outdoor exercise area. Water bottles are inexpensive and can be purchased in all pet supply shops. They are usually sold as rabbit bottles but work very well for puppies and grown dogs. Using this procedure will eliminate the water mess on your kitchen floor as well as reducing staining by keeping your dog's beard dry.

Your puppy's first **collar and leash** should be very soft and made of a lightweight leather or nylon. The collar should be tight enough not to slip over the head but loose enough to easily place two fingers under the collar. When collar-training, do not use a choke collar; it could very easily catch on a protruding object and strangle your puppy or dog.

After a few days with the collar training, attach a leash to the collar and allow the puppy to run free with the collar and leash attached. Do this a few minutes at a time for several days. I suggest you supervise this procedure and correct the puppy if he tries to chew on the leash. Within a few days, your puppy should be quite willing to walk with you without objecting to the collar and leash. We have always considered the Bichon extremely easy to lead-train. (See Chapter 8, "Basic Training," for more information on training your Bichon.)

Safe Toys

Like babies, puppies teethe. I'm certain you would rather your puppy chew on a rawhide bone than your furniture, kitchen cabinets or woodwork. Buy the rawhide bone with a knot tied at each end rather than the chewsticks, for they can cut the mouth. Soft squeaky rubber toys are adorable but can be hazardous as well as expensive. The little metal piece that makes the squeak usually comes out, and the puppy can easily swallow it and suffer serious consequences. Hard rubber toys are safe and extremely durable. You can also tie knots in old socks or dishtowels for them to play with and these toys are easily kept clean—just toss them in the washer.

The plastic tops off of spray cans are one of my Bichons' favorite toys. The tops roll on the floor, making quite a bit of noise, and when they pick them up, the tops flip over their noses. However, if the plastic edges become jagged, discard them immediately.

Identification

How many "lost pet" signs have you seen posted or listed in the newspaper? Every day pets are lost. It is highly recommended that your pet have some type of identification as soon as possible. Although your yard may be secure, a child or meter-reader may accidentally leave the gate open.

Millions of pets never make it back home because they are not identified! Many are destroyed in animal shelters or, even worse, they are sold to laboratories for research and testing.

The very least expensive means of identification is an "**ID tag,**" which is a tag with the owner's name, address and phone number either printed or engraved and attached to the pet's collar. When somone finds a lost dog, the tag is the first, perhaps even the only, thing they look for. The only problem with this method is your dog may lose his collar, in which case the tag will be lost with it. For this reason, it's important to have a more permanent method of identification as well.

A **tattoo** is another means of identification. Inquire through your veterinarian or local all-breed kennel club about locating a tattoo clinic for dogs. Your dog's AKC registration number or your social security number will be tattooed on the inside flank of the hind leg. The tatooing is minor and is not painful to your dog.

The newest identification device is the **microchip,** a tiny computer chip that has an identification number programmed into it. The entire microchip is small enough to fit into a hypodermic needle and is injected under the skin. This provides a lifetime identification that cannot be lost or removed. The procedure is not painful and your pet does not have to be sedated.

Puppies can be "identified" during their initial vaccine series. In the future, all veterinarians and animal control shelters will have a scanner to read the identifications that have been programmed into the microchips, though at present these services are not widely available.

Bed or Crate

Every dog deserves to have a bed of his own—a snug, warm spot where he can retire undisturbed when he wishes to nap or sleep through the night.

A crate is useful as a training tool and a secure haven for your puppy, or puppies, in this case.

With a small puppy, it is desirable to have the bed arranged so the puppy can be securely confined at times, safe and contented. This is why a dog crate is the ideal bed for your dog. It offers not only security and privacy, but it is also a great asset in housebreaking. These crates are available in most pet supply stores. A number 100 is the recommended size for your Bichon puppy. When he's grown, you may find the number 200–size crate to be more comfortable for him.

Suddenly being taken from his mother and littermates can be a frightening experience for your puppy, but with your understanding and common sense, the shock can be softened. Naturally, for the first few nights he's alone, your puppy will be lonely and cry and perhaps howl! If he does, put him in his crate and

place the crate next to your bed at night. If he cries during the night, just touch the crate to assure him that you are there and he is not alone. Speak to him in a firm but gentle tone.

Bichon puppies love to snuggle up to a soft, stuffed toy animal, and if the animal happens to be white and fuzzy, so much the better! This becomes a temporary mother and littermate substitute. Also, to simulate the mother's heartbeat, you can put a loud ticking clock in his bed. Wrap the clock in a soft cloth before placing it in his bed.

At this point I must admit that most Bichons—young or old, pet or show dogs—usually sleep with their owners, and they readily attach themselves to children and delight in joining a child in bed, but this is a decision to be made by each individual owner.

Never use his crate as a form of punishment; doing so would be defeating its purpose. He should be taught that the crate is his own little den. He will want to keep it clean and will automatically go to it when sleepy or when he wants to get away from the outside world. Place a towel and a favorite toy or rawhide bone inside the crate. During the day keep the crate in the busy part of the house, for the Bichon needs to feel like he is one of the family and wants to know what is happening at all times. Keep the crate door open to enable him access. When you leave the house or will be out of the room for a while, put the puppy in the crate and secure the door. This way, you not need worry, for both the puppy and household furnishings are safe.

A Schedule for Your Puppy

We mentioned in the last chapter that schedules are important for Bichons, and for puppies in particular. Having a new puppy in the house is an exciting, life-changing thing, but the kindest thing you can do for your puppy is to minimize this extraordinary change and set up a normal life as soon as possible. Try to feed and walk your puppy at tne same times each day. Remember your puppy's cycles will be quite short; he will eat, sleep, play, relieve himself and do it all over again in an hour or so.

After he eats, plays or gets excited he will need to go outside. As he gets older, of course, he'll be able to go longer between naps and potty trips. If you are consistent and responsive to your puppy's needs and training, he will turn into the model young adult (see Chapter 8 for complete information on basic training).

Puppy Food

Reputable pet food manufacturers have spent many years learning to formulate the food required for all stages of dogs' lives. Your puppy should be fed a well-known brand of dry kibbled dog food that is nutritionally balanced and meets the needs of puppies during their period of rapid growth and development. You will not need to purchase canned dog food or milk for your puppy.

(For more on this subject see Chapter 5, "Feeding your Bichon Frise.")

This Bichon puppy will grow into a cheerful and well-adjusted adult with the right training and attention from her owners.

Traveling with Your Bichon

When traveling with your Bichon, make sure he has fresh water available and a toy or two. It is safest if you contain him in a seat belt made for dogs or in his crate.

If a car accident were to occur, the crate would act as a safety barrier, and he'd have less of a chance of being seriously harmed or thrown from the car. Always have his crate placed in an area easily accessible to you, with his leash attached to the crate.

Even though Bichons can become well-seasoned and well-adjusted little travelers, there may come a time when he should not accompany you on a trip. This is certainly the case when the weather is too hot for him to travel. You may have to stop, rest or go into a restaurant, and during this break your Bichon cannot be left alone in the car—not even with the windows cracked! (See Chapter 7 for more information on heatstroke.) It is also never advisable to leave your Bichon in an unattended car unless you can see him, because he may be stolen.

Boarding Your Bichon

When your Bichon friend cannot be included in your travel plans, you must seek proper care for him during your absence. There are many options available, and you must do research before placing your Bichon into anyone's care.

"In home" pet care may be an option in your area. The obvious advantages to this service are that your dog is neither in a strange environment nor is he being exposed to other pets that may be ill or harboring fleas.

The disadvantage may be that he will be bored or feel deserted and may potty in the house or even destroy your furniture! Some in-home care organizations have personnel who will stay in the house around the clock with your pet, but do you want a stranger in your home? Other "in home" pet services send personnel to your home several times a day (feeding time, exercise time) leaving your pet unattended for long periods of time. If you choose "in home" care, find out what experience the caretaker has. Are they qualified to perform first aid if it's needed? Can they recognize need for medical care? Do they know how to keep your Bichon's coat tangle-free?

Another option is **boarding at the vet's.** It is our opinion as breeders, exhibitors, and pet owners that vet clinics should never board healthy pets unless they have separate facilities to house them from the sick pets. A separate facility must include a separate heating and air-conditioning unit, so as not to spread airborne viruses. The dogs should never be exercised or watered in the same area as the ill pets.

One advantage of using **boarding kennels** is that you will not have strangers in your home. When seeking a boarding kennel for your Bichon, you must go see the facilities for yourself. Look for a clean building containing both an inside and outside concrete run for your pet. Only use a kennel that requires proof of shots. In addition to the yearly shots and rabies, they should also require that their boarders have a kennel cough preventative administered before entering.

Does the staff seem caring and genuinely interested in your dog's needs? Seek a boarding kennel that has someone on the grounds twenty-four hours. The best kennels' proprietors or managers live on the premises. Call your vet, groomer or breeder and ask about the kennel's reputation. If they are evasive and suggest a different kennel—take their advice. While vets never want to badmouth a kennel, they should be able to readily recommend a good one!

Because your breed, the Bichon, requires special coat care, make sure the kennel offers professional bathing or grooming services. A brush-out as well as baths will need to be scheduled for extended stays. Use the kennel that will adhere to your feeding, medicating and coat care instructions. If they are not writing these instructions down upon "check in," I doubt they have any intention of following them.

Because Bichons are quite adaptable and easily trained they are usually good little boarders. But you must

PUPPY ESSENTIALS

Your new puppy will need:

food bowl

water bowl

collar

leash

I.D. tag

bed

crate

toys

grooming supplies

prepare your dog as well. Most kennels offer day boarding for a nominal fee, and this is the best method of familiarizing your Bichon with the kennel. When leaving your Bichon for the day, be sure to pack some treats and his favorite toys. After doing this several times, your Bichon will become accustomed to his surroundings and will be ready for an overnight stay. Usually one or two occasional overnighters are sufficient. If you only travel once or twice a year, plan his adjustment stays approximately seven to fourteen days prior to the actual extended stays and he will understand the routine and may even enjoy his stay. Always leave your vet's telephone number and a number at which you can be reached with the kennel staff.

Good kennels will discuss how your pet will be boarded with them. During these reports listen and ask questions, so you can ensure your pet's stay is not traumatic. If he did not eat well, find out why. Was he too excited or depressed? In either case, you may need to provide the kennel with his favorite foods from home to entice him to eat during his next stay.

If he was depressed, then he was not getting enough individual attention and you will need to sign him up for a walk time or play periods. Most kennels offer these extra services for an additional charge, but if they don't, other arrangements can usually be made. Per-haps a friend or relative could come by a few times and visit and walk him. Good boarding kennels bend over backward to make the pet's stay comfortable and pleasant, and are more than willing to help you with any special needs.

One drawback to a boarding kennel is that your pet may get kennel cough during his stay, even if he has been inoculated against it. Kennel cough has so many strains that there are not enough inoculations available to cover them all! It is hard to prevent kennel cough from hitting a boarding kennel because it is airborne, and it takes seven to nine days after the dog has been exposed before he even comes down with any symptoms! Fortunately, kennel cough is not life-threatening and is easily cured. Never blame or expect the kennel to pay vet bills concerning kennel cough, for it is not their fault. It is very much like sending your child to school, where he or she will certainly catch some kind of bug!

chapter 5

Feeding Your Bichon Frise

The Elements of a Good Diet

The essentials of your dog's diet are protein, carbohydrates, fats, vitamins, minerals and water. If your dog is to grow properly and look and feel good, each of these elements in the correct amount must be included in his daily diet. Too little or too much of any of these nutritional necessities can be harmful.

Some people feed the very best food and then give their Bichons that extra dose of vitamins "just to be sure." This is not beneficial, and in fact is quite dangerous. Too much can cause a harmful reaction in a dog's system. When considering your Bichon's diet, everything good in moderation is to be remembered.

PROTEINS

Proteins are found in fish, meat, milk, eggs, cheese and some beans. They are needed for essential body building. Twenty to thirty percent of your dog's meal should be protein, depending on age and activity. Growing puppies require extra protein.

CARBOHYDRATES

Carbohydrates should make up between 50 and 70 percent of your dog's dinner. They are found in grains and sugar. Carbohydrates give energy and growing power. Unused carbohydrates are stored under the skin as fat. If you fill your dog up with carbohydrates, he won't eat the protein he needs to keep him healthy. It would be like eating a large dessert before dinner time.

FATS

Fats are important in a dog's daily ration. Fat acts as a vitamin reserve and aids digestion by slowing the passage of food through the intestines. Fat also keeps his coat healthy and shiny. Fat provides twice as much energy as an equivalent amount of carbohydrate or protein, but too much fat will cause diarrhea. Your family pet requires no more than 5 percent fat content, though working dogs require more. If you find your dog's coat and skin a bit dry, add one to two teaspoons of vegetable oil to his meal two or three times a week.

TYPES OF FOODS/TREATS

There are three types of commercially available dog food—dry, canned and semimoist—and a huge assortment of treats (lucky dogs!) to feed your dog. Which should you choose?

Dry and canned foods contain similar ingredients. The primary difference between them is their moisture content. The moisture is not just water. It's blood and broth, too, the very things that dogs adore. So while canned food is more palatable, dry food is more economical, convenient and effective in controlling tartar buildup. Most owners feed a 25% canned/75% dry diet to give their dogs the benefit of both. Just be sure your dog is getting the nutrition he needs (you and your veterinarian can determine this).

Semimoist foods have the flavor dogs love and the convenience owners want. However, they tend to contain excessive amounts of artificial colors and preservatives.

Dog treats come in every size, shape and flavor imaginable, from organic cookies shaped like postmen to beefy chew sticks. Dogs seem to love them all, so enjoy the variety. Just be sure not to overindulge your dog. Factor treats into her regular meal sizes.

Vitamins

A certain amount of vitamins is essential in your pet's diet. When using a high-quality-brand dry food, it is not necessary to add supplemental vitamins and minerals.

Minerals

Minerals are also found in many foods and do not need to be supplemented unless there is a specific need for more. Minerals such as calcium and phosphorus are used to build bones and teeth and are found in milk, eggs, vegetables, liver and cereals. The higher-quality dog foods contain calcium and phosphorus in properly balanced amounts. Be careful not to add excessive calcium, especially without the proper percent of phosphorus. A dog can actually suffer a deficiency of calcium without the phosphorus. If calcium is prescribed, use a product made specifically for dogs.

Canned or Dry Food?

The highest-quality canned dog food is quite expensive, considering that most kinds contain 70 to 85 percent moisture (in other words, water). It is easy to prepare; a can opener is all you need. Yes, it would be quite a simple way to feed your dog, but it is a totally unacceptable method.

The most popular and proven way to feed your dog is a high-quality dry food that can be fed dry or moistened, or mixed with a very small amount of meat, vegetables, cottage cheese, etc. Just remember, dry dog food is the main diet. Most dog food manufacturers even claim that adding a supplement to their dry food (vitamins, mineral supplements or another food) can upset the perfect nutritional balance of their product. However, we do feel that a small amount of added food is healthful and appealing to the taste buds. Given a proper diet, a Bichon should not experience flatulence, unlike some other breeds that appear prone to this problem.

Feeding Your Bichon Puppy

Just how much do you give a puppy? At certain times during a puppy's growth, she will require nearly twice the amount of most nutrients per pound of body weight as an adult dog. At about eight weeks of age, a puppy requires as much as three times the adult caloric requirements per pound of body weight. When your puppy reaches four months of age, the amount gradually decreases to the adult requirements, which of course vary according to the puppy's breed. We find that our three- to four-month-old Bichon puppies require about one and a quarter to two cups of dry food per day. We do add small amounts of chopped chicken, cottage cheese or cooked vegetables such as carrots or green beans. At this age they weigh approximately six to seven pounds. This amount of food is divided into two or three feedings.

A daily dog biscuit helps in teething, as does a medium-size rawhide bone (made in USA only). No chew sticks please, they are capable of cutting the inside of the puppy's mouth. I have also heard of a chew stick becoming lodged in a dog's throat, so I do not recommend them. A medium-size rawhide bone with a knot at each end should be quite safe.

Very young puppies can be fed all the food they want—at their scheduled meal time. About the time you take your puppy home (eight to ten weeks) you can feed him the dry puppy formula either on a self-feeding program or begin with scheduled feedings three times a day. I suggest you discuss this with the puppy's breeder or your veterinarian.

TO SUPPLEMENT OR NOT TO SUPPLEMENT?

If you're feeding your dog a diet that's correct for her developmental stage and she's alert, healthy-looking and neither over- nor underweight, you don't need to add supplements. These include table scraps as well as vitamins and minerals. In fact, a growing puppy is in danger of developing musculoskeletal disorders by oversupplementation. If you have any concerns about the nutritional quality of the food you're feeding, discuss them with your veterinarian.

Feeding Your Older Bichon

While a free-feeding program may be all right for the active, adult Bichon, your elderly Bichon may have a tendency to eat more than he needs. To keep your older Bichon in top shape, an adjustment of his regular feeding program will probably be necessary. Use the same brand of high-quality dry kibble you've been feeding, and switch to the formula made especially made for older dogs. If you've been free-feeding your Bichon, it's time to offer fixed amounts of food one or two times a day.

Keeping your older Bichon active and monitoring his food intake will help prevent obesity. Carrying too much weight is not only unattractive, but unhealthy as well and can shorten your Bichon's life.

Don't give in to the appealing expressions dogs put on when trying to get some of your meal.

Don'ts to Remember

Never feed your dog or puppy chicken bones, pork bones or fish bones. Your pet can choke on these bones, and if one were swallowed, it could require surgery and could even be fatal. Raw eggwhite should never be fed, since it cannot be digested by the dog and may cause diarrhea.

Hearts and livers are excellent in nutrition but easily cause diarrhea and upset stomach. Give them in very small amounts.

Pork in any form is forbidden. Too much fat at a given time is upsetting and cannot be digested. Indiscriminate use of vitamins and minerals are unjustified and may actually be harmful. No milk should be given once your puppy is weaned. Milk will cause loose stools and it is no longer needed. Candy and people snacks are taboo. Once you start giving your dog sweet snacks and salty treats such as potato chips, it will immediately become a habit and as soon as he hears the crinkle of a snack bag, he will start to whine and beg. Dogs love salt! To avoid possible kidney and bladder problems later in your dog's life, it is wise to avoid this. Remember, chocolate can be deadly to dogs! Also taboo are fried foods, highly seasoned foods and extremely starchy foods, for the dog's digestive tract is not equipped to handle them.

Water

Have water available at all times, though you may wish to restrict how much water a puppy gets just before bedtime. Choose a place for the food and water bowls away from the household traffic and noise. Remember the previous tips given concerning the water bottles (see Chapter 4, "Bringing your Bichon Frise Home.")

Self-Feeding Program

Self-feeding means always keeping dry food available so your dog can

HOW TO READ THE DOG FOOD LABEL

With so many choices on the market, how can you be sure you are feeding the right food for your dog? The information is all there on the label—if you know what you're looking for.

Look for the nutritional claim right up top. Is the food "100% nutritionally complete"? If so, it's for nearly all life stages; "growth and maintenance," on the other hand, is for early development; puppy foods are marked as such, as are foods for senior dogs.

Ingredients are listed in descending order by weight. The first three or four ingredients will tell you the bulk of what the food contains. Look for the highest-quality ingredients, like meats and grains, to be among them.

The Guaranteed Analysis tells you what levels of protein, fat, fiber and moisture are in the food, in that order. While these numbers are meaningful, they won't tell you much about the quality of the food. Nutritional value is in the dry matter, not the moisture content.

In many ways, seeing is believing. If your dog has bright eyes, a shiny coat, a good appetite and a good energy level, chances are his diet's fine. Your dog's breeder and your veterinarian are good sources of advice if you're still confused.

eat as much as he wants at any given time. For a small dog, such as a Bichon, keep a fresh cup of dry food in his bowl. Never add fresh food to the left-over food. The dry food in his bowl should be fresh and kept in a clean bowl.

Some breeders feel this is a lazy and dirty way to feed—we do not agree. Bichons are active, playful house dogs and we seldom find that our young dogs are inclined to overeat. Yes, the more senior dogs often do require restrictions on the amount of food given. Along with this method of self-feeding, we offer a small moist meal in the early evening. Suggestions for this meal follow.

A high-quality dry food will contain all the nutritional elements your Bichon needs to keep her happy and healthy.

Moist Meal

½ to 1 cup of dry food mixed with *one* of the following:

Chopped chicken

Cottage cheese

Tuna

Cooked scrambled egg

Cooked vegetable (chopped)

Mix thoroughly

We suggest you do not feed wet and sloppy foods. This type of food encourages loose stools and will hasten dental problems, including unhealthy gums and tartar build-up.

Weight Problems

We are all very conscious of weight. Not only should we watch our own weight but our pets' as well. I have been told by a veterinarian that dogs can eat up to 50 percent more food than they require and still act hungry. Dogs weighing between fifteen and twenty-five pounds need about 1,000–2,000 calories per day.

If your dog is on the heavy side, you will have to restrict his diet and increase his activity. This may be as simple as reducing the amount of food, or you can offer a similar amount of a food lower in calories. On the market today there are dog foods available for every possible phase of a dog's life: for puppies, working dogs and even the overweight or senior dog. Make certain your puppy is fed puppy-formula dry food, adults are fed the formula specifically for adults, and geriatrics are fed food formulated especially for them.

HOW MANY MEALS A DAY?

Individual dogs vary in how much they should eat to maintain a desired body weight—not too fat, but not too thin. Puppies need several meals a day, while older dogs may need only one. Determine how much food keeps your adult dog looking and feeling her best. Then decide how many meals you want to feed with that amount. Like us, most dogs love to eat, and offering two meals a day is more enjoyable for them. If you're worried about overfeeding, make sure you measure correctly and abstain from adding tidbits to the meals.

Snacks

Are you being stared at by soulful eyes? Is every bite you eat at dinner followed by your dog? Do you give in and slip him "just a bit" to keep him happy and show you care? *Don't* if you want your dog to have good manners and, more important, to remain healthy.

A well-fed, well-trained dog eats only what you put in his dish. Encouraging dogs to eat other foods from other sources makes them "dinner-pests," and begging food from other people could be harmful. A guest could unwittingly give improper or even dangerous food to your dog. If your dog continues to beg and make a nuisance of himself, perhaps he is truly hungry and has not been given the proper diet or amount of food. It is wise to double-check your pet's diet and see that it contains the essentials he needs to be truly fit and healthy.

chapter 6

Grooming Your Bichon Frise

The Bichon Frise is a high-maintenance dog in the grooming department. This breed requires extensive care in order to maintain its well-known and charming "powder-puff" look. Don't let this dissuade you from owning a Bichon; you can sacrifice the powder-puff look and opt for a low-maintenance haircut or style. Both the longer, more traditional trim and the shorter trim will be covered in this chapter.

Equipment

First let's discuss what equipment will be needed to keep your Bichon neat, tidy and free of parasites and skin problems: medium-size oval wire pin brush, small slicker brush, stainless steel Belgian comb, nail clippers (I prefer the guillotine type), styptic powder, hemostats with a blunt tip, ear powder, alcohol, cotton balls, soft toothbrush and tooth scaler, blow-dryer, good quality shampoo, two or three large towels, table with nonskid surface, professional 8-inch haircutting scissors.

The Bichon's Coat

The adult Bichon has a double coat. This simply means that he has an outer coat and an undercoat. The undercoat is soft and silky. At maturity the outer coat has a harsher texture because of the guard hairs. The soft puppy coat starts getting guard hairs around the age of six months and you will notice this happening first on the lower back. During this change your puppy will need frequent brushing so the coat does not become matted. Dematting is not only time-consuming, but it is also uncomfortable for the puppy. The easiest thing to do is prevent it.

Save the pin brush for areas with the longest hair, like the head and tail.

Brushing and Combing

The coat must always be brushed and combed through thoroughly before bathing. If mats get wet, the hair gets tighter, making de-matting next to impossible. When it's time to brush or bathe your dog, always do it on a nonslip surface. Some people use the washer or dryer and place a bath mat on top.

The dog needs to be taught to lie down on his side for the brushing and drying sessions. This can best be accomplished by getting on the floor with him, patting the floor and giving him the "lie down" command. You will need to gently lift him and ease him onto the floor. Once he is in the correct position, begin to gently stroke him. Then you can introduce him to the raised area you will use as the grooming table. Practice the "lie down command" several times and remember—*lavish him with praise.* This is a training session, not punishment time!

Once you and your Bichon have mastered this feat, you both are ready for the brushing. First, start with the slicker brush. Save the pin brush for the tail, neck and head area. With the dog on his side, use the slicker brush, getting all the way to the skin. Never brush the coat of a Bichon with long strokes, for this only fluffs the outer coat. I prefer brushing from the hip area, moving up toward the neck. Once I have reached the neck area I stop and save this area for the pin brush. Remember, the pin brush is for the area with the longest hair.

After you have brushed the legs, tummy, sides and chest with the slicker brush, start doing the remaining area with the pin brush. Take small sections of hair and get all the way down to the skin. If you do hit a mat, try to break it up with your fingers. Once you have pulled it apart, hold the mat in one hand and brush it with the other. When you feel that the mat has been removed, then comb out the area of the mat, and ensure that the entire mat is indeed removed. After the entire body is brushed, you will need to comb through the dog. Again, do not take long strokes over the top of the coat. Lift the hair so you can see a section of the dog's skin and start combing as close to the skin as possible, pulling the comb to the very ends of the coat. This is the true test as to whether you have removed all mats. After you've gotten familiar with the proper brushing and combing methods, the length of this session should be approximately ten minutes. The

Bichon needs a thorough brushing two to three times a week.

Ears

Now you're ready to do ears. As long as your Bichon has clean, healthy ears, they only need attention once a month, but should be checked weekly during your brushing session.

Bichons grow long hairs inside their ears! You or your groomer must remove this hair. While the dog is on his side, shake some ear powder into the ear canal. This provides a coating on the hair so it can be removed with ease. Once the hair is coated, begin pulling it out gently with the hemostats. Take small amounts at a time so as not to hurt him. If done properly once a month, this will not be an unpleasant experience.

After all hair has been removed from the ear canal area, it is time to clean the ear. Apply alcohol to a cotton ball and squeeze out the excess amount. Use the cotton ball to swab out the entire ear. If there is a reddish-brown color accompanied by an odor, the dog probably has an ear infection. If this is the case, please refer to Chapter 7, "Keeping Your Bichon Healthy."

Nails

Nails need to be trimmed on a monthly basis. When your dog is walking on a slick surface, you should not hear her nails clicking along the floor. Before trimming your dog's nails, make sure your nail clippers have a nice sharp edge and that styptic powder is nearby. Start by lifting the dog's foot so you can see a profile of her nails. If the nail is clear or light in color, you will be able to see the quick. Cut the nail to just before the quick. If you cut too deeply, the nail will start to bleed. If this happens, coat the end of the bleeding nail with styptic powder until the bleeding stops. If the nail is black and you cannot see the quick, clip only the tip of the hooked part of the nail. Take care not to squeeze the dog's paws too tightly when trimming nails, for this will cause discomfort that she'll associate with nail trimming.

Do not forget to cut your dog's dewclaws if she has them. Dewclaws are located on the inside front and rear leg, near the dog's wrist area. Most breeders have dewclaws removed when the pups are a few days old. It's acceptable to some breeders to leave front dewclaws intact, but rear dewclaws on the Bichon are never acceptable.

Trimming Foot Pads

While it's not mandatory that you learn to trim your Bichon's foot pads, we do recommend it. This hair will be trimmed by your groomer, but what if your grooming appointment has been delayed? Keeping this area free of hair not only helps traction, it also gives the owner an opportunity to make sure the dog hasn't picked up any thorns, rocks or other debris.

To trim pads, lift the foot, and spread the pad with one hand. Trim almost flat with the scissors. Never put the point of the scissor into the pad! Leave about 1/8 to 1/4 inch of hair.

GROOMING TOOLS

- pin brush
- slicker brush
- flea comb
- towel
- mat rake
- grooming glove
- scissors
- nail clippers
- tooth-cleaning equipment
- shampoo
- conditioner
- clippers

Teeth

Two or three times per week your Bichon will need to have his teeth brushed. Using a child's soft toothbrush dipped into a paste of water and baking soda, start by brushing gently from the gumline in a downward motion. If your Bichon has healthy gums they will be firm and pinkish in color. If they bleed and are red and swollen, please refer to Chapter 7, "Keeping Your Bichon Frise Healthy."

If your dog fights a toothbrush, use a piece of gauze wrapped around your finger and dipped into the paste. With this method, you must rub vigorously to remove tartar.

You may also need to use the tooth scaler. Always take the edge of the scaler and grab the top part of the

tartar and with a quick downward movement try to "scale" the tartar off the tooth. If the tartar is not coming off you will need to ask your groomer or veterinarian to remove this before tooth decay or gum disease occurs.

Bath Time

So your Bichon needs a bath? Assuming he's in the traditional pet clip, in which the hair on his neck and head are longer than the coat on his body, you will start by holding his muzzle upward and wetting his head, exercising great care not to get water down his throat or nose. The Bichon's coat is like a thirsty sponge and it takes time to get it good and wet. After wetting the dog thoroughly, apply a shampoo recommended for white dogs. Gently squish the shampoo into the coat. Do not scrub! This will cause matting. When you get to the eye area, we recommened using a tearless shampoo. After sudsing, be sure to rinse thoroughly, as shampoo residue will cause dry skin and itching.

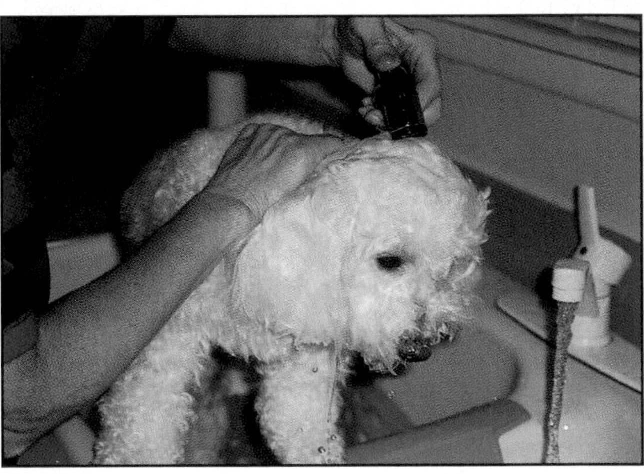

Bichons need frequent bathing to keep them white and clean.

After rinsing, squeeze excess water from the dog and wrap him in a thick towel. Remove him from the tub, place him onto a clean dry towel and begin to blot and squeeze him dry. After squeezing him dry, discard the wet towel and partially wrap him in a dry towel, exposing his head only.

Now you will need to **blow-dry** your Bichon's coat. On the medium setting, begin to blow-dry your Bichon's head, taking care the dryer is not too hot! From the head continue down the neck and entire back. Remember—no long strokes over the top of the coat. Take a small section of hair and continue brushing and drying until there are no crinkles. Remove any wet towels and continue to blow-dry the rest of the dog's body. If your dog has a thick hardy coat you may dry him with the slicker brush and switch to the pin brush for the head, neck and tail. If his coat is brittle or silky you should use the pin brush on the entire dog. While blow-drying, do not skip around; finish drying the entire head before continuing to the neck and beyond.

After rinsing your Bichon thoroughly, wrap him in a thick towel to absorb excess water.

Once your Bichon is dry you will need to comb his entire coat. During this final combing, you will "fluff" him, for this is how the "powder-puff" look is achieved. When combing each section of hair, pull the comb off the body. This makes the coat stand off the body.

Now review your result. Does he look curly? If so, you did not dry each section of hair thoroughly or you dried the section without enough brushing. Brushing while drying straightens the coat.

Never bathe a coated Bichon and let him dry naturally, and never crate-dry a Bichon. Crate drying means a dog is contained in a wire crate with a dryer hooked to it. If you do not blow-dry the Bichon, his coat will dry kinky, resulting in an unkempt look and a tendency to mat.

Give your dog lots of praise and affection during grooming sessions.

Pet Trim

The most popular pet trim on a Bichon is done by clipping his body close, leaving one-half inch of coat. His neck and head are left slightly longer. This "summer short" style is easy to maintain and requires fewer trips to the groomer. The pet owner who opts for the longer, traditional trim will need to have his dog scissored professionally every four to six weeks; Bichons can go eight to ten weeks between grooming appointments when trimmed in the shorter style. Another advantage to the summer short is that the owner can bathe and blow-dry his dog in about twenty minutes!

Regardless of trim, your Bichon will need to be bathed at least every three weeks. If your dog is exceptionally active outdoors, following the children to play, helping you plant flowers or walking on the beach, you may find that he needs a weekly bath.

Shortcuts

Don't have the time to bathe him and company is coming? Unless he is wet or muddy, he can be spruced up in five to ten minutes and look just fine. Shake baby powder or a similar powder into his coat and pat it in. Then brush the powder into the coat. Voilà! Whiter, fresher and very poofy! Make sure you powder him outside or in your tub so the powder doesn't get everywhere.

A well-groomed Bichon in any trim style looks healthy and attractive.

During the flea season you may need to wash your Bichon in a flea-killing shampoo. Have your vet or groomer recommend a safe product. Flea products dry out the coat and the skin, so a good cream rinse will be required. If the fleas have caused sores on the skin, the dog will require two shampoos—one to kill the fleas and a medicated shampoo to soothe the skin.

chapter 7

Keeping Your Bichon Frise Healthy

Choosing a Vet for Your Bichon

Your vet should be someone that makes you feel your Bichon's health is a priority for him as well as yourself. Choose a clinic that is immaculate and in which the staff appears well-trained and helpful. If your puppy was purchased locally, ask the breeder for a reference, or ask friends and neighbors who they use and why. Never establish your Bichon as a client if you feel you are being hurried in and out of the clinic. Look for a vet who is gentle and thorough and will take the time to explain issues to you. During routine exams, you should be allowed in the examining room with your Bichon. Watch your vet as he or she goes over your pet—is he listening to your dog's heart? Has he checked his ears, nose and throat? This is the best time for you to establish a relationship with your vet, so don't hesitate to ask any questions. Get your vet's opinion on your Bichon's general health. Find out if you are overlooking or neglecting any needed care.

Preventive Care

There are some easy steps you can take to help make sure your Bichon stays in good health throughout his life. As well as saving your pet infinite discomfort, these preventive steps will save you money and heartache in the long run.

When you are snuggling or grooming your Bichon, take a few minutes to run your hands over him. Feel for any bumps, sores, or anything out of the ordinary. Be attentive to how much he eats and drinks and the way he moves when he exercises. Changes may signal that something's wrong, and early detection can save lots of trouble.

YOUR PUPPY'S VACCINES

Vaccines are given to prevent your dog from getting an infectious disease like canine distemper or rabies. Vaccines are the ultimate preventive medicine: they're given before your dog ever gets the disease so as to protect him from the disease. That's why it is necessary for your dog to be vaccinated routinely. Puppy vaccines start at eight weeks of age for the five-in-one DHLPP vaccine and are given every three to four weeks until the puppy is sixteen months old. Your veterinarian will put your puppy on a proper schedule and will remind you when to bring in your dog for shots.

Vaccinations

An easy way to keep your pet from contracting some of the most dangerous diseases is to vaccinate. Determine a schedule with your veterinarian and stick to it!

Vaccines are killed or modified live forms of the diseases you are trying to prevent. The mild form of the disease stimulates the immune system to produce antibodies. Some antibodies are passed to puppies via their mother's milk. These maternal antibodies can sometimes interfere with the effectiveness of vaccines, so puppies are not inoculated until they are totally weaned.

When you purchase your Bichon puppy, he should already have started his series of puppy shots. If not,

seek a different breeder. Ethical breeders will never send their puppies to a new home without at least one inoculation. This series is usually given every two weeks and your vet clinic will set the shot schedule for your pup. The most common series is three sets of combination shots given at two-week intervals, followed by one more combination shot after the age of twelve weeks. Rabies shots are given between the ages of four and six months, depending on the state you live in.

When you bring your puppy home, she should already have had some of her first shots. You need to continue her inoculations.

After your puppy is a year old, he'll get one annual booster throughout his life to prevent canine infectious diseases. The rabies inoculation may be given in two forms—an annual booster or a rabies shot good for three years. Again your vet will help you to schedule your Bichon's inoculations.

Some people are sadly misinformed and feel that because their dog never leaves the house and is never exposed to other canines, he doesn't need shots. Not so! Some diseases are airborne viruses that you may bring home on your clothes or your dog may acquire in his own backyard! So please keep your Bichon's inoculations current!

Distemper Life-threatening, particularly for the very young or the elderly Bichon. The symptoms for distemper are similar to a severe cold, and progress to neurological problems. It is highly contagious.

Hepatitis This virus attacks the liver and kidneys, and causes bloody diarrhea and high fever. Life-threatening and contagious.

Leptospirosis Leptospirosis damages the kidney and liver and causes loss of appetite, fever, vomiting and diarrhea. Advanced stages produce lesions on the tongue and gums.

Parainfluenza (Tracheobronchitis, kennel cough) Treatable. To this date, there are more strains of this virus than there are vaccines. The most common name for this virus is kennel cough. It takes seven to nine days after a dog has come down with kennel cough before any symptoms appear. Symptoms are a hacking cough and spit-up consisting of yellow, foamy phlegm.

Parvovirus This virus is life-threatening and extremely dangerous. Diarrhea and vomiting are the most common symptoms. Dehydration occurs rapidly.

Coronavirus Symptoms are the same as in parvovirus, and it is likewise life-threatening. However, unlike parvovirus, coronavirus is not always included in the combination shot series, so make sure your vet offers it at some point.

Rabies Always fatal, and may be transmitted to humans. It is carried by wild animals such as skunks, squirrels, fox and bats. Rabies may infect any warm-blooded animal, including humans.

Spaying and Neutering

Another easy way to keep your pet in the best of health is to spay or neuter it. In fact, we cannot stress enough the importance of having your pet spayed or neutered. One only has to go to the local pound or S.P.C.A. to see the tremendous number of unwanted and homeless animals. The majority of these abandoned animals were once somebody's pet, but our disposable society seems to dispose of pets as well! If all dogs and cats throughout the world were spayed or neutered, we would not have the pet overpopulation problem that we are experiencing today.

In addition to the moral issues, pet overpopulation causes many problems for all people—animal lovers or not. Pet overpopulation can inflate the incidence of

dangerous diseases, such as rabies, that can be spread to humans. And what about the astronomical amount of money that is needed to house, feed, and care for these unwanted animals? What about the cost of euthanizing the abandoned animals that are too sick, too old, or too hard to place?

Spaying Your Female (Ovariohysterectomy)

The benefits of spaying your female Bichon are numerous. Besides the obvious (not producing puppies), there are many health benefits. The risk of mammary (breast) cancer in a spayed bitch is reduced by 95 percent.

She is also safe from pyometra, a life-threatening uterine infection. Bitches suffering from pyometra may stop eating and become very lethargic and depressed. They may drink large amounts of water and urinate frequently.

Spaying will also prevent many vaginal infections. The most common sign of a vaginal infection is a discharge and perhaps some staining of the coat around the vulva. Protrusion of the vagina (vaginal prolapse) occurs when a bitch is in heat. The vulva becomes painfully enlarged due to the amount of estrogen being produced. When the vagina keeps swelling, it will eventually protrude through the vulva, causing considerable pain. It is generally a recurring problem, and when she comes in heat again, chances are she will have vaginal prolapse again.

> **ADVANTAGES OF SPAY/NEUTER**
>
> The greatest advantage of spaying (for females) or neutering (for males) your dog is that you are guaranteed your dog will not produce puppies. There are too many puppies already available for too few homes. There are other advantages as well.
>
> **ADVANTAGES OF SPAYING**
>
> No messy heats.
>
> No "suitors" howling at your windows or waiting in your yard.
>
> Decreased incidences of pyometra (disease of the uterus) and breast cancer.
>
> **ADVANTAGES OF NEUTERING**
>
> Lessens male aggressive and territorial behaviors, but doesn't affect the dog's personality. Behaviors are often owner-induced, so neutering is not the only answer, but it is a good start.
>
> Prevents the need to roam in search of bitches in season.
>
> Decreased incidences of urogenital diseases.

In addition to the many health benefits of spaying, there are many conveniences as well. During the

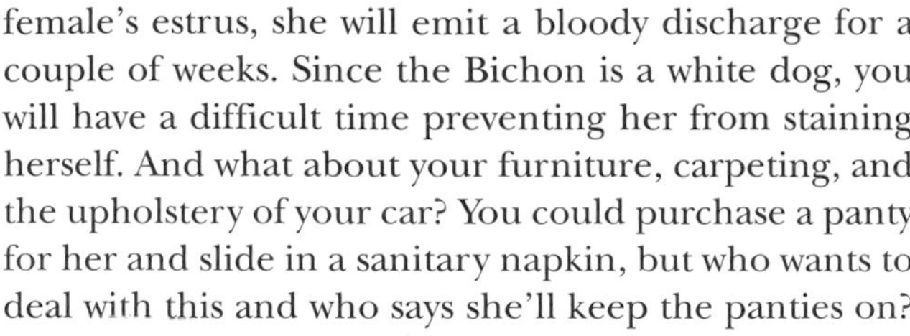

female's estrus, she will emit a bloody discharge for a couple of weeks. Since the Bichon is a white dog, you will have a difficult time preventing her from staining herself. And what about your furniture, carpeting, and the upholstery of your car? You could purchase a panty for her and slide in a sanitary napkin, but who wants to deal with this and who says she'll keep the panties on?

Spaying or neutering will **not** *make your Bichon overweight. Every dog needs a proper diet and plenty of exercise to remain in top shape.*

While your bitch is in heat, she is attracting every intact (not neutered) male for miles around! Some males' mating drive is so strong they will scale your fence to get to your bitch. Males will mark their territory by urinating all over your car tires, shrubbery and even your doors! And forget taking your bitch for a walk while she's in heat—you'll feel like the Pied Piper, and some males can get quite aggressive if you try to deter them from their love interest.

There are some myths regarding spaying. One such myth is that she will become fat or even obese. This is a myth. Obesity occurs when dogs are overfed, underexercised or have a health problem, like a thyroid disorder, that causes weight gain.

Another myth is that she should have a litter of puppies before she is spayed. Again we repeat, **this is a myth!** Most dogs today are very domesticated, especially Bichons, whose only purpose has been that of a companion dog. Mother Nature tells bitches to procreate when they are in estrus; it's a chemical, not psychological, instinct. An ovariohysterectomy removes the uterus, tubes and ovaries of the bitch and along with them the hormonal drive to breed. Human companionship is what your Bichon desires.

So now that you have decided to spay your bitch, what's the best way to proceed? Make sure her inoculations are current, and make sure she's not in season. If she is, the cost of the procedure will increase and it will be more difficult for your Bichon and your vet.

When making your appointment, follow pre-surgery procedures explicitly. This will entail withholding food and water the night before surgery. Failure to withhold food and water may cause your Bichon to vomit during induction of anesthesia, which can be dangerous.

Prepare yourself to be without your Bichon friend for one night, as most vets require an overnight stay after surgery. Schedule the surgery to coincide with a day that you can stay with her on her first day home. Be informed of postoperative procedures. Most vets will send you home with written instructions. If your Bichon does not seem to be herself on her second day home, alert your vet!

Neutering Your Male (Castration)

Neutering your male has health benefits as well. Your neutered Bichon is not susceptible to prostate cancer. Males prone to urinary tract infections will exhibit less stressful bouts of this because of the absence of the prostate. Neutering your male will also prevent testicular cancer.

Neutering your male will make him a calmer pet and you a happier owner. If he's neutered before puberty, his sexual desires never develop, and this is quite a bonus for it greatly reduces his desire to roam. Bichons are housedogs and they need to be easy to live with. Neutering your male makes him easier to housebreak. Male dogs lift their legs to urinate, but they also lift their legs to mark their territory. Once neutered, he will have less of an urge to mark his territory.

Follow the same preoperational procedures you would for the female. However, most males do not require an overnight stay at the vet's.

Maintenance

You can make sure all your Bichon's parts are in working order by taking a few minutes to maintain them. Clean and properly maintain your Bichon's teeth, ears, eyes and anal glands to help prevent serious problems from developing.

Teeth Puppies, like babies, are born without teeth. The juvenile or deciduous teeth begin to appear at the age of four or five weeks. The permanent teeth come in at approximately four to five months of age. During the teething period, your puppy may drool and his gums may become tender, causing him to go off his food somewhat. Make sure you provide him with many chew toys during this time, and offer him a soft toy as well as his rawhide bone. During the teething time, it is wise to check the Bichon's mouth to make sure he is not retaining his baby along with his adult teeth. If a baby tooth is still visible after the adult tooth has erupted, you will need to have your vet remove it.

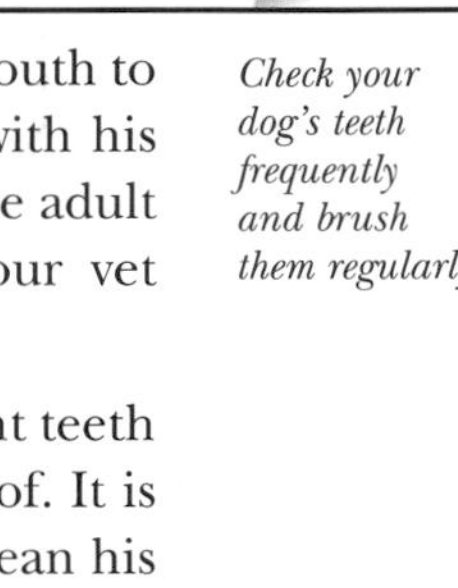

Check your dog's teeth frequently and brush them regularly.

Bichons have a tendency to lose their permanent teeth at an early age unless the teeth are taken care of. It is never too late to train your Bichon to let you clean his teeth. Start by rubbing your fingers over his teeth and massaging his gums. Once he is comfortable with this you can wrap your finger with gauze and rub his teeth vigorously to prevent tartar build-up. After the gauze technique has been mastered, you may introduce a toothbrush. Use a child's soft brush or purchase one made specifically for dogs. There are commercial dog toothpastes on the market that come in many "doggy" flavors such as beef or liver. If you don't choose a commercial brand of dog toothpaste, make your own by simply mixing a little water into some baking

soda. Never use human toothpaste of any kind on your Bichon!

Feeding your dog dry food and offering him biscuits or hard dog cookies helps clean the teeth. If your water is hard, you may find that you need to brush his teeth frequently; usually two to three times per week is sufficient. If your Bichon has staining on his teeth, you can help lift the stain by swabbing the teeth with a 3 percent hydrogen peroxide solution.

If you brush your puppy's teeth on a routine basis, he should never get heavy tartar build-up. If he does, you will need to use your tooth scaler. Take the tip of the tooth scaler, go just above the area of tartar build-up and with a downward motion scale the tartar off. Take caution as not to hit his gums—the scaler is sharp! If this is not successful, you may need to ask your vet to remove the tartar for you. An ounce of prevention goes a long way in good oral hygiene, for it will increase the life of your dog's teeth and help to keep him in good health in his advanced years. Remember—this is a long-lived breed.

Because the Bichon is a heavily-coated breed, you must take care to scissor hair away from the eyes.

Periodontal disease begins as gingivitis. If your Bichon's gums are soft and bright red, your friend needs a trip to the vet immediately. The vet may put your Bichon on an antibiotic before he or she can actually treat the painful gums. Advanced stages of gingivitis may require that your Bichon be anesthetized for treatment and he may lose some teeth as well!

Ears Because the Bichon is groomed and bathed frequently, you shouldn't have a problem with ear infections. Every time your Bichon is bathed, his ears should be cleaned (see Chapter 6, "Grooming Your Bichon Frise.")

Suspect an ear problem if your Bichon starts holding his head to one side or shaking his head frequently. Other signs are a bad odor from the ear, redness, swelling or discharge. If your Bichon has any of these symptoms, you will need to take him to the vet. These symptoms can indicate a fungal infection, mites or any one of a number of possible problems. You must get your vet's diagnosis.

Mites are tiny white bugs that live in the ear canal eating skin debris. They are highly contagious, so if your Bichon lives with another pet they will both need to be treated at the same time. Your vet will swab the ear canal and examine the specimen under a microscope. Treatment is done on a daily basis for approximately three weeks. An antibiotic is prescribed if mites are complicated by an additional bacterial infection.

Eyes If your Bichon's eyes become watery and he squints and paws at them, find out what the cause is. To examine the eye, you will need a good source of light. Place one thumb below your Bichon's eye and the other above on the ridge of the bone. Gently draw down with your lower thumb. If you see nothing, lift the eye gently from above. If you see a piece of hair or dirt, you can remove this with a moistened towel. If this does not remove the foreign object, you may need to gently flush the eye out with tepid water. If the eyelids are inflamed, red and thick-looking, your Bichon will require medicine from your vet. Never use human eye ointment on your Bichon without first asking your vet.

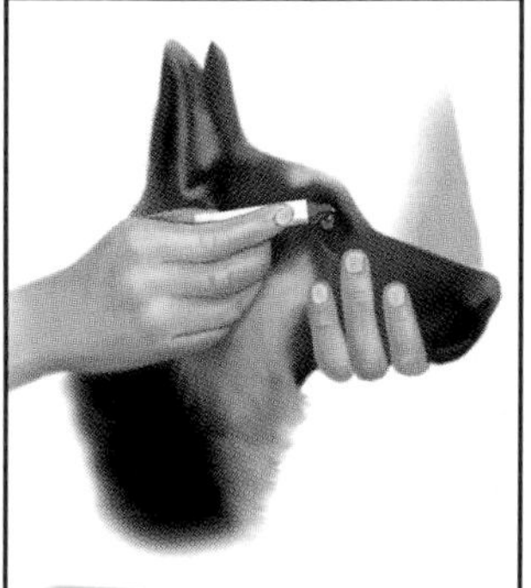

Squeeze eye ointment into the lower lid.

Because your Bichon is a heavily coated breed, you must exercise caution in keeping hair from his eyes.

Most groomers charge a very small amount to scissor this area between his regular grooming appointments and you can wait while it's being trimmed.

Some Bichons tear, which causes a red strain under the eye. Constant trimming of this area helps prevent the stain from setting in. If staining occurs, take a 3 percent solution of hydrogen peroxide on a cotton ball and swab the area daily.

Nose Your dog's nose should feel cool and moist. If your Bichon starts sneezing and has a runny nose, you will need to observe him to see if other symptoms develop. If his nose becomes warm and dry to the touch, he may have a fever.

A constant clear discharge may indicate a nasal irritation. Nasal irritations may be caused by foreign objects or allergies. If your dog has a thick discharge coming from the nose accompanied by mucus in his eyes, you have a very sick Bichon who needs to be taken to the vet.

Bichons seem to be prone to "reversed sneezing." This usually happens when the Bichon becomes very excited or very anxious. He will produce a loud snorting sound as if something is lodged in his nose and he's trying to draw it in. While this "attack" sounds violent, there is no cause for alarm. It won't last more than one minute, though it seems like a lifetime to the owner. Your Bichon will catch his breath on his own, but if you want to assist you can cover his nostrils to force him to take a breath or two through his mouth.

Anal Glands Dogs have two anal glands or sacs located at about five and seven o'clock on the circumference of the anus. The healthy, properly fed Bichon will empty these glands during defecation. The anal gland secretion is brownish or creamy looking and has a foul odor. If your Bichon becomes extremely stressed or frightened, he may accidentally empty these sacs. Most dogs do not need to have their anal glands expressed manually unless there is some medical reason to do so. In our experience, Mother Nature and a proper diet take care of it. When establishing a groomer for your Bichon, please request that your Bichon's glands not be emptied on a routine basis; once they are emptied manually Mother Nature gets lazy. However, if your Bichon is constantly cleaning his anus and scooting his hindquarters across the floor, they just may need to be emptied.

While raising the dog's tail, take a warm washcloth and locate the glands. They feel like small, firm bumps. Grasp the skin on the outside of the sacs with your thumb and forefinger and push and squeeze them together. If the discharge is bloody, your Bichon has an infection and will require veterinary care.

Taking Your Dog's Temperature

Taking your Bichon's temperature is easier today than it was in years past because we now have digital thermometers that give a reading in a matter of seconds. A healthy dog's temperature is approximately 101 degrees Fahreinheit. To take your dog's temperature, you will need petroleum jelly and a rectal thermometer.

If there are two people it is much simpler. Have your assistant hold the front end of the pet while you grasp his tail and insert the well-lubricated thermometer into his anus. If you are by yourself, it is a little difficult, but you should be able to manage. Have your dog stand on his grooming table and take one arm and go over his back and reach your hand under his tummy while drawing him close to your body. With your free hand, insert the thermometer.

Medicating Your Bichon

If you have medication in a **liquid form** to administer to your Bichon, chances are he will not take this willingly! Most medicines do not take into consideration that your Bichon has gourmet taste buds! This is simplified by using an oral syringe and inserting it into the back corner of his lips while holding his mouth closed. Keep the head tilted back and the muzzle closed until he has swallowed.

If the medication is in **pill form**, it is usually easier to get down. If he is an eager eater, you may simply roll his pill into a favorite treat such as peanut butter or cheese. This method is fine as long as you are positive he has not eaten the treat and spit out the pill! If this method is not working for you, the pill must be manually administered. This is easiest on the grooming table. Grasp the upper part of his muzzle, intentionally positioning his lips to cover his teeth; he will be less inclined to close his mouth. Open his mouth wide, and place the pill as far back on his tongue as possible. Once the pill is inserted, hold his mouth shut while tilting his head back. With your other hand, gently but firmly stroke his throat until you feel him swallow. Make sure he truly has swallowed the pill and not just pushed it out the side of his mouth. Check thoroughly to make sure the pill isn't hidden in his beard! Praise your Bichon once the pill is down or he may believe he did something to displease you. Offer him a healthy treat or play with him so he doesn't associate pill-taking with any displeasure.

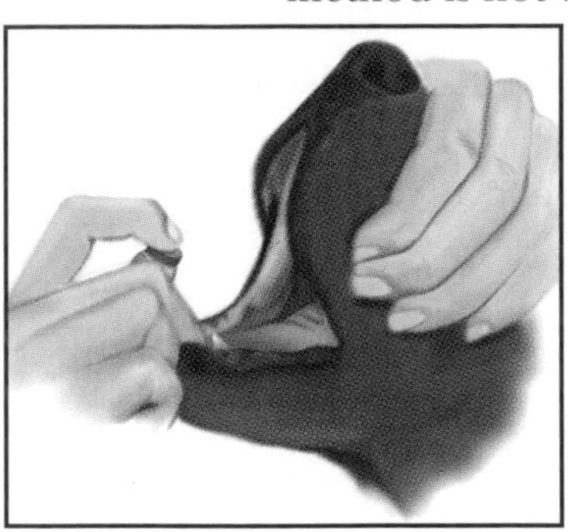

To give a pill, open the mouth wide, then drop it in the back of the throat.

Internal and External Parasites

Internal

If you feel that your Bichon is having frequent off-days or just doesn't look as robust as usual, suspect an internal parasite. Take a stool specimen to your vet. Usually they can give you the results in ten to fifteen minutes. Leave your Bichon at home when you go—the less exposure to ill pets the better. If your vet finds a parasite, he or she will prescribe the proper medicine and dose. You can administer the de-worming medicine yourself.

Most dogs will get worms at some time in their life. There are numerous worms that infect dogs. The most common are roundworms, tapeworms, hookworms and whipworms. Some people are horrified at finding out their Bichon has worms and associate worms with filth. Not so, as we will explain.

Roundworms are present in almost all puppies even when the dam (mother) was wormed just prior to being bred. This worm causes a dull coat and potbelly, as well as loose stools, coughing and diarrhea. If roundworms are left untreated, the infected dog may start passing these worms in the stool and will become very lethargic. Though not preventable, your vet can prescribe effective de-worming medicine.

Tapeworms are the most common internal parasite in both puppies and adults. This worm is also the largest—as long as several feet! Yuck! They live in the small intestine and the head of the parasite attaches itself to the wall of the gut. Tapeworms cause a dull coat and loss of weight. If you notice a speck that looks like dried rice around the anal area you have discovered that your pet has tapeworms. Your Bichon can get tapeworms from ingesting a flea that has eaten tapeworm eggs, or by eating raw or uncooked meat. Since fleas are the most common host for the tapeworm, you will not only need your vet to prescribe the proper deworming medicine, but you will also need to de-flea your Bichon to prevent reinfestation.

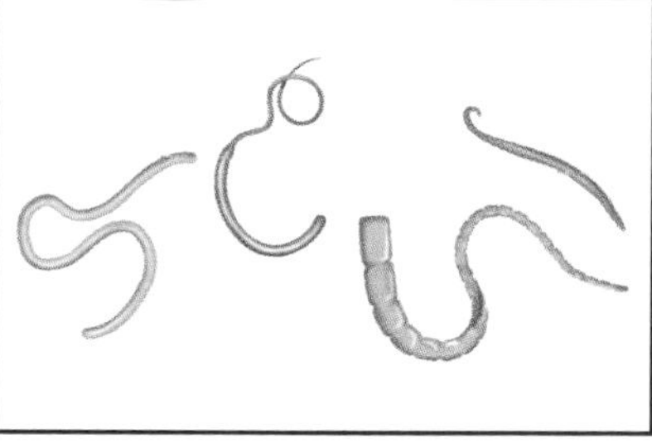

Common internal parasites (l-r): roundworm, whipworm, tapeworm and hookworm.

Hookworms are small, thin worms that attach themselves to the intestinal walls and suck the host's blood, causing anemia. The infected Bichon will have pale, whitish gums and dark stools that look like tar. Puppies can acquire this worm in utero, before they are born. This worm can be in contaminated soil in your yard or park. The dog becomes infected by coming into contact with the contaminated soil or contaminated feces. If you are treating your Bichon for hookworm infestation, remember to pick up his stools frequently and sprinkle a little lime over the area he soiled. The lime helps to keep the soil clear. Again, contact your vet for the proper de-worming medicine.

Whipworms are thin, small worms that look like a tiny, two-inch-long whip with one end thicker than the other. This worm lives in the large intestine. Whipworms cause dogs to lose weight, have loose stools and an unhealthy look. This worm is sometimes very hard to detect and it may take several stool samples before showing up. Dogs can get whipworms from soil heavily contaminated with eggs.

Please note that you must always have your vet prescribe the proper de-worming medicine. Never use over-the-counter de-worming capsules on your pet. They may cause severe stomach distress and may not be effective for the type of worm your dog is harboring. Get in the habit of poop control on a daily basis.

Heartworms infect your dog's circulatory system and heart. Heartworms will kill your Bichon. They are carried by mosquitoes, and it only takes one bite from the infected mosquito to infect your dog! There really is no excuse for any dog being infected with heartworms in this day and age. Heartworms are preventable and your vet will start your Bichon on a pill to do just that. There are two kinds of heartworm preventative pills: One is given on a daily basis, while the other is administered once per month.

Symptoms of heartworm include inactivity, lethargy, exhaustion, and a quiet nonproductive cough. Your Bichon will need to be tested for the presence of heartworms before he is placed on the preventative program, but once he is, you can be assured that he will never be infected by them! An ounce of prevention is often the best medicine.

FIGHTING FLEAS

Remember, the fleas you see on your dog are only part of the problem—the smallest part! To rid your dog and home of fleas, you need to treat your dog *and* your home. Here's how:

- Identify where your pet(s) sleep. These are "hot spots."
- Clean your pets' bedding regularly by vacuuming and washing.
- Spray "hot spots" with a non-toxic, long-lasting flea larvicide.
- Treat outdoor "hot spots" with insecticide.
- Kill eggs on pets with a product containing insect growth regulators (IGRs).
- Kill fleas on pets per your veterinarian's recommendation.

External Parasites

Fleas are parasites that live on your dog, biting it and ingesting the blood. Many dogs are allergic to the flea's saliva and will scratch and irritate the flea bite until a sore develops. Bichons are *very* sensitive to fleas. They will scratch and bother the bite, ruining their coats and developing painful and unsightly sores. It's imperative for the owner to keep fleas under control all the time.

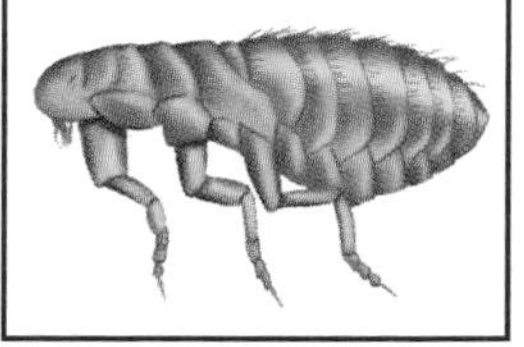

The flea is a die-hard pest.

In order to keep your dog free of fleas, you have to rid the dog and its environment of these pests. Flea eggs remain in the carpet or yard and will reinfect your dog as soon as they hatch. Bathe your dog with a flea shampoo; vacuum the carpets and treat the yard. If they are left anywhere, your dog will immediately be reinfected.

There are many flea-killing products available, both chemical insecticides and natural substances. Ask your veterinarian or groomer for suggestions about the best product to use. Whichever one you choose, be sure to read and follow the directions carefully. Some products contain strong chemicals and you should take care when using them.

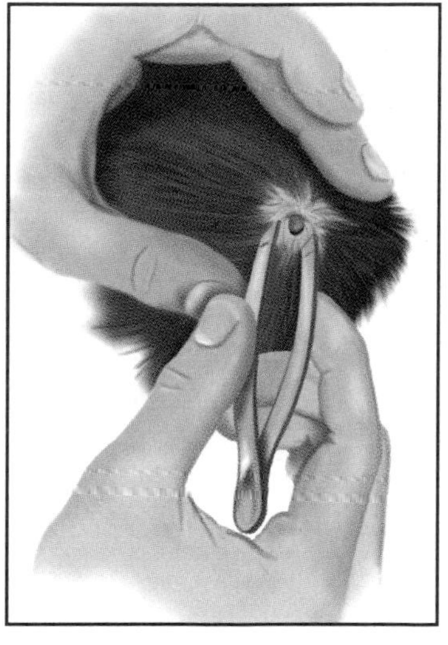

Use tweezers to remove ticks from your dog.

Ticks attach themselves to your dog and ingest its blood. They usually prefer the area around the ears, head or neck. Ticks carry all kinds of diseases, including Lyme disease and canine ehrlichiosis.

The best way to remove a tick is to dab it with alcohol or nail-polish remover a few moments before attempting to detach it. This should kill it, or at the very least, make it loosen its

grip. Then grasp the tick with tweezers as close to your dog's body as possible. Pull it off and check to make sure you've removed all of it. To kill it, burn it or put it in a container of alcohol. Clean the bite with antiseptic ointment. The best way to keep ticks under control is to check for them often, especially after walking in wooded or grassy areas in the spring or summer when they are most prevalent.

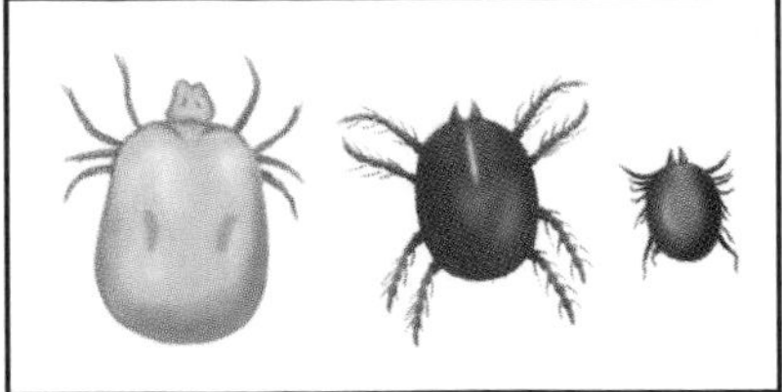

Three types of ticks (l-r): the wood tick, brown dog tick and deer tick.

Emergency Situations

If you have established a good working rapport with your vet and staff, they can help you to decide over the phone whether your Bichon should be seen by the vet. They may ask you what his temperature is in addition to questions such as what his stools look like and what or when he has last eaten. Be organized and have as much information at hand as possible before calling their office. Your vet may advise you over the phone how to take care of the problem, thus saving you a medical bill as well as an unnecessary trip. If your Bichon needs to be seen by the vet, your phone call was not wasted because the clinic is now alerted to your problem before you arrive.

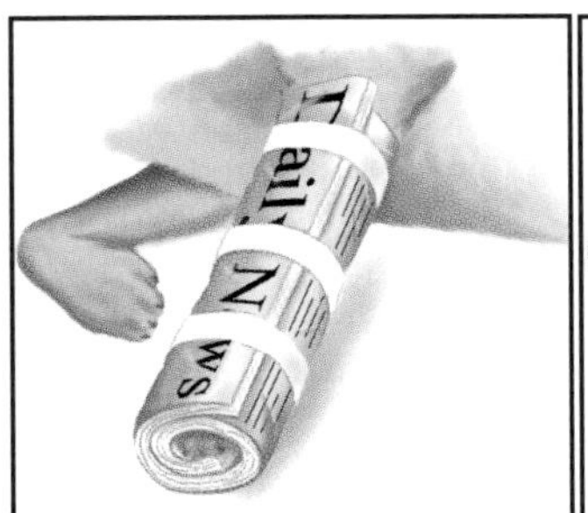

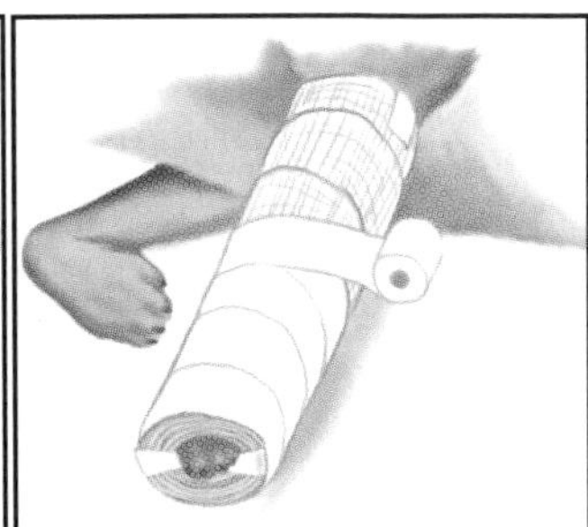

Make a temporary splint by wrapping the leg in firm casing, then bandaging it.

Call your vet if your Bichon is not eating, has diarrhea, fever or is vomiting. These can be indications of a severe condition, or just an upset stomach, so call your vet before taking emergency measures. If your Bichon is restless or has his back arched, he is in pain, probably in the abdominal region, and he will need to be seen immediately.

Accidents If your Bichon is injured by an automobile or from a fall, this will warrant a trip to the vet. Approach the injured Bichon with caution, for he may not be himself and may bite. Be prepared to muzzle him with a piece of cloth or women's hosiery by wrapping and tying it around the dog's muzzle. Keep the animal quiet and warm during and before transport. If the Bichon does not seem to need to bite or lash out, then do not muzzle him, because he may be having difficulty breathing. Even if your Bichon doesn't seem injured after this mishap, take him to the vet. He may have internal injuries that are life-threatening!

Run your hands regularly over your dog to feel for any injuries.

Bleeding Apply direct pressure to the wound or use a tourniquet, depending on the location of the wound. When using a tourniquet, remember to release the pressure periodically to avoid cutting the circulation off too long. These are methods of first-aid only and you still need to take your Bichon to the vet.

Poison Many seemingly harmless substances are extremely toxic to dogs. One of the most common accidental poisonings occurs when dogs ingest antifreeze. This is usually lethal unless you witnessed the dog lapping it and are lucky to live close to your vet. Etheneglycol is the toxic ingredient in most antifreezes, but fortunately there are now brands on the market that do not contain this

Some of the many household substances harmful to your dog.

ingredient, making for a safer product around your Bichon.

Certain plants are toxic to your Bichon. Unfortunately, they seem to be popular houseplants! We will list a few here, but you will need to do further research.

Toxic Houseplants:

Amaryllis

Asparagus fern

Bird of paradise

Azalea

Elephant ears

Umbrella plant

Most variations of ivy

Pot mum

Toxic Outdoor Plants:

Delphimium

Daffodil

Skunk cabbage

Mushrooms

Morning glory

Wisteria

Foxglove

Larkspur

Jasmine

Periwinkle

Toxic Trees and Shrubs:

Apricot

Almond

Peach

Cherry

English holly

Japanese plum

Mock orange

Wild cherry

Some of the above toxic plants are hallucinogens; some will produce sores in your Bichon's mouth and others will cause vomiting, diarrhea, seizures, coma and death. If you think your Bichon has ingested any of the above, seek medical help as soon as possible!

Shock Lack of adequate blood flow will cause your Bichon to go into shock. The signs of shock are shivering, a weak pulse, cold feet and legs, listlessness, and pale skin or gums. Blanket the dog and transport him to the vet immediately. If he is unconscious, make sure he can breathe by clearing secretions from his mouth with your fingers and pull out his tongue to keep his airway free. Keep his head lower than his body and transport him to the vet immediately.

Artificial Respiration If your dog has stopped breathing, you will need to give artificial respiration. Open mouth and clear away secretions. Lay the dog on his side with his right side down. Next, pull the tongue forward and close the mouth while sealing the lips with your hand. Place your mouth over the dog's nose and blow into the nostril for three to four seconds. The chest should have expanded—now release it. Transport the dog to a vet, continuing to repeat above steps until he breathes on his own.

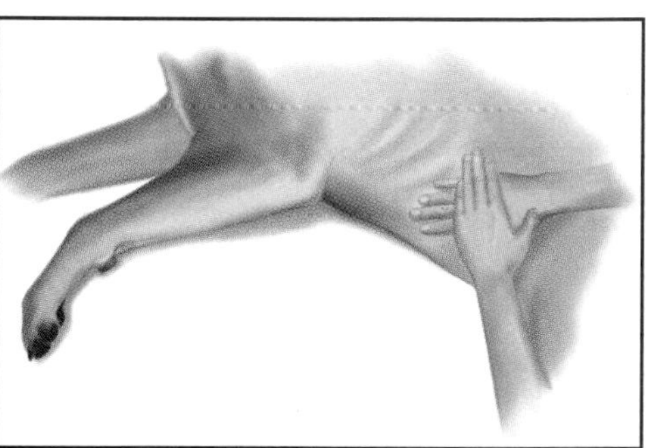

Applying abdominal thrusts can save a choking dog.

If your dog is **drowning,** you will have to administer artificial respiration. First, hold the dog upside down by his hind legs to let the water run out of his windpipe. Position the head lower than the body, and begin artificial respiration.

Heatstroke This is life-threatening and requires first aid even before you get to the vet. Heatstroke occurs when a dog becomes overheated and his body temperature becomes elevated. He will begin to stagger or stand perfectly still; his pupils will be dilated. He will be panting and his sides will be heaving heavily. His tongue may be bright red or purple. You must act quickly to save his life! Start by bringing his temperature down while someone starts the car and has the air-conditioning going. Run cool water over his body, or, if a tub is available, submerge him in cool water. For a temperature of 106 degrees or higher, give him a cold-water enema. When he seems to be less stressed, wrap him in a wet towel and transport him to the vet.

Avoid situations that could cause your Bichon to overheat. Never take him for a car ride in hot weather if your vehicle is not air-conditioned. Never take your Bichon with you when you are running errands, for you cannot leave him in the hot car! If you live in a hot climate and do not have air-conditioning, the Bichon is not for you. They do not do well in hot weather and can be prone to heat stroke—especially if they have a long coat. Never take them to the beach during hot weather.

A FIRST-AID KIT

Keep a canine first-aid kit on hand for general care and emergencies. Check it periodically to make sure liquids haven't spilled or dried up, and replace medications and materials after they're used. Your kit should include:

- Activated charcoal tablets
- Adhesive tape (1 and 2 inches wide)
- Antibacterial ointment (for skin and eyes)
- Aspirin (buffered or enteric coated, *not* Ibuprofen)
- Bandages: Gauze rolls (1 and 2 inches wide) and dressing pads
- Cotton balls
- Diarrhea medicine
- Dosing syringe
- Hydrogen peroxide (3%)
- Petroleum jelly
- Rectal thermometer
- Rubber gloves
- Rubbing alcohol
- Scissors
- Tourniquet
- Towel
- Tweezers

Diarrhea This is a reaction or a symptom, not an illness, so remember to address the illness as well as the diarrhea. If you know the cause for the diarrhea, you can help the problem. While it is not advisable to use human medication on your Bichon, there are exceptions to the rule and treating diarrhea is one of them. Pepto-Bismol or Kaopectate may be given in small doses (via oral syringe) two to three times a day, depending on how bad the diarrhea is and how he is responding to it. Make sure you get the syringe down his throat as explained in the section on "Medicating Your Bichon" earlier in this chapter. Pepto-Bismol stains the Bichon's coat, so take precautions to avoid this.

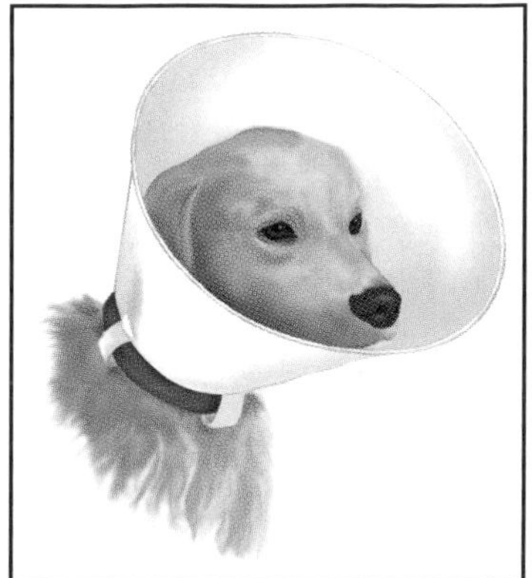

An Elizabethan collar keeps your dog from licking a fresh wound.

You can help control loose stools and diarrhea through your Bichon's diet. Boiled chicken meat with no fat and broth over rice is an excellent meal for your Bichon with diarrhea. You can simplify this by giving him chicken noodle or chicken and rice soup. This will be all he will need for a day or two while his tummy settles. If the diarrhea persists after two days, consult your vet.

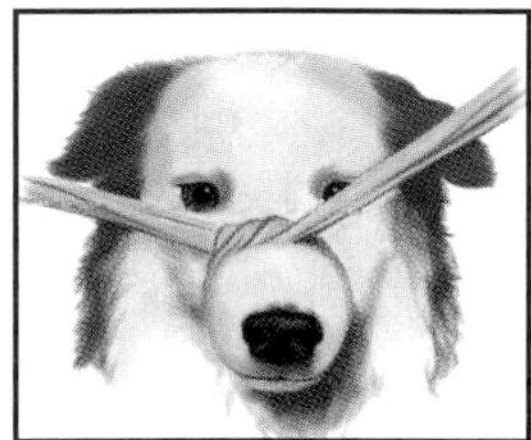

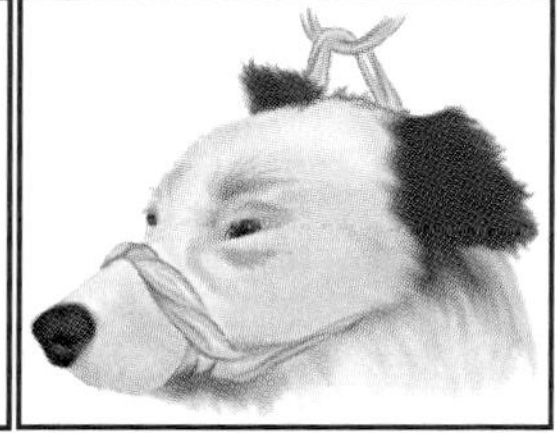

Use a scarf or old hose to make a temporary muzzle, as shown.

On the other hand, if your Bichon has a hard time producing his stool, you will need to examine it. Is it hard and dry? If so, he may need more fiber in his diet, and there is also the possibility that he is not drinking enough water. You can also try adding just a little under a teaspoon of cooking oil for a day or two mixed into his main meal.

Regularly check your pet's stool by just looking at it. You do not have to touch it or poke at it! Your Bichon's stool will tell you many things about his health. Checking his stool frequently will give you some idea

as to whether he has internal parasites. Roundworm and tapeworm segments may readily be seen in the stool, and blood or mucus in the stool may indicate the presence of a different kind of internal parasite.

Hot Spots Some Bichons are prone to hot spots. Hot spots are red inflamed patches anywhere on your Bichon's body. If left unchecked, they will become infected and require a vet trip. Sometimes these are caused by flea bites. If this is the problem, you need to address the flea situation immediately (see "External Parasites" in this chapter).

When you see a hot spot starting, swab the area with hydrogen peroxide. While still damp from the peroxide, apply cornstarch directly to the affected area. The peroxide cleans up the area and the cornstarch dries up the sore. Discourage him from cleaning or chewing this area. Be stern and tell your Bichon "No!" If he continues, mist the area with Bitter Apple, or a similar product. If your Bichon continues to develop hot spots, and doesn't have fleas, have your vet refer you to a canine skin specialist.

WHEN TO CALL THE VET

In any emergency situation, you should call your veterinarian immediately. You can make the difference in your dog's life by staying as calm as possible when you call and by giving the doctor or the assistant as much information as possible before you leave for the clinic. That way, the vet will be able to take immediate, specific action to remedy your dog's situation.

Emergencies include acute abdominal pain, suspected poisoning, snakebite, burns, frostbite, shock, dehydration, abnormal vomiting or bleeding, and deep wounds. You are the best judge of your dog's health, as you live with and observe him every day. Don't hesitate to call your veterinarian if you suspect trouble.

Problems Particular to the Bichon Frise

Tooth Loss Proper dental care has already been discussed earlier, but this is a good opportunity to reiterate the importance of it. Bichons seem to be more prone to tooth loss than other breeds, so great care must be taken to keep the mouth in good condition. Brush your dog's teeth at least three times a week and follow up with professional examinations at regular intervals.

Bladder Stones Bichons and other small breeds are somewhat more susceptible to bladder stones than larger breeds. Talk to your veterinarian about possible dietary elements that may contribute to their formation. Also, be sure your Bichon is not confined in a situation in which he is forced to hold his urine. Be sure someone is available to let your dog out often.

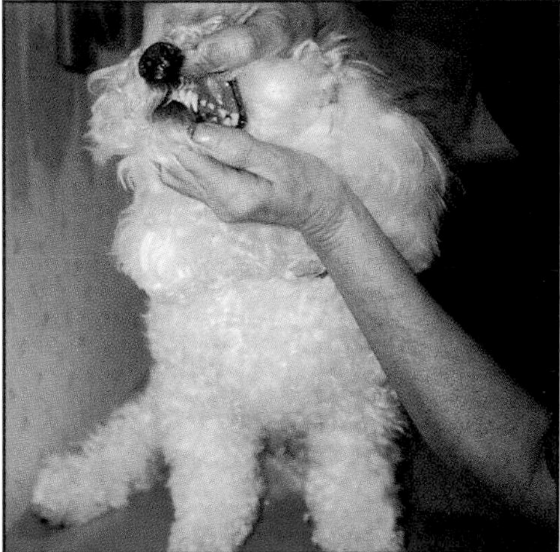

Bichons can be prone to dental problems. It's very important to brush the teeth regularly and follow up with professional care.

Symptoms may include frequent and bloody urination and general weakness and fatigue. If you suspect a bladder stone, take your Bichon to the vet as soon as possible. If left untreated, they can cause kidney damage and death.

The Bichon is basically a hardy little dog with a healthy appetite and a zest for the good life. When in a happy home environment, he is not prone to neuroses seen in some other breeds. He is neither hyper nor anxious—he is simply an active, playful dog. Bichons are clean and are very intelligent; one only needs to look into his dark eyes to see how smart and merry he is.

Old Age and Euthanasia

The Bichon is a long-lived breed, and relatively free of the genetic problems that plague some breeds. If given the proper health attention at home and by the veterinarian, he will live a long and healthy life.

However, you will have to make some adjustments as he ages. The older Bichon will want to eat more and exercise less. Don't let him! This could create a weight problem with unhealthy consequences. (See Chapter 5 for more information on feeding your older Bichon.)

Make sure you continue to exercise your Bichon, though this may mean a leisurely walk around the block instead of three exuberant laps around the park. Adjust his exercise program to suit his body's changing needs, but never forgo activity altogether. Not only does excercise help prevent obesity, it helps to reduce joint stiffening and it gives your dog the quality of life he deserves. As he grows older, he still needs the stimulation that a look at the world outside your home provides.

Your older Bichon may experience arthritis. If stiff joints seem especially painful, consult your veterinarian. He or she may prescribe painkillers.

Your older dog may also start to lose sight and hearing. Remember this when it seems like he's not listening to you.

Eventually a time will come when the bad days outnumber the good for your elderly Bichon. Your dog depends on you to make decisions concerning his well-being and this last one is no exception. Ask your vet for advice, but don't let him or her make the decision about euthanasia for you. You alone are qualified to judge when the quality of life of your Bichon has deteriorated beyond acceptable limits.

Once you have made this difficult decision, it is also up to you to execute it well. Go with your dog to the vet's office, and reassure him while the veterinarian administers an overdose of anesthetic. Talk gently and lovingly to your dog, and as he falls to sleep the last thing he will remember is your love.

IDENTIFYING YOUR DOG

It's a terrible thing to think about, but your dog could somehow, someday, get lost or stolen. How would you get him back? Your best bet would be to have some form of identification on your dog. You can choose from a collar and tags, a tattoo, a microchip or a combination of these three.

Every dog should wear a buckle collar with identification tags. They are the quickest and easiest way for a stranger to identify your dog. It's best to inscribe the tags with your name and phone number; you don't need to include your dog's name.

There are two ways to permanently identify your dog. The first is a tattoo, placed on the inside of your dog's thigh. The tattoo should be your social security number or your dog's AKC registration number.

The second is a microchip, a rice-sized pellet that's inserted under the dog's skin at the base of the neck, between the shoulder blades. When a scanner is passed over the dog, it will beep, notifying the person that the dog has a chip. The scanner will then show a code, identifying the dog. Microchips are becoming more and more popular and are certainly the wave of the future.

Your Happy, Healthy Pet

Your Dog's Name ______________________________

Name on Your Dog's Pedigree (if your dog has one) ______________________________

____

Where Your Dog Came From ______________________________

____

Your Dog's Birthday ______________________________

Your Dog's Veterinarian

Name ______________________________

Address ______________________________

Phone Number ______________________________

Emergency Number ______________________________

Your Dog's Health

Vaccines

type ______________________________ date given ______________

type ______________________________ date given ______________

type ______________________________ date given ______________

type ______________________________ date given ______________

Heartworm

date tested __________ type used ______________ start date ______________

Your Dog's License Number ______________________________

Groomer's Name and Number ______________________________

Dogsitter/Walker's Name and Number ______________________________

Awards Your Dog Has Won

Award ______________________________ date earned ______________

Award ______________________________ date earned ______________

part three

chapter 8

Basic Training

by Ian Dunbar, Ph.D., MRCVS

Training is the jewel in the crown—the most important aspect of doggy husbandry. There is no more important variable influencing dog behavior and temperament than the dog's education: A well-trained, well-behaved and good-natured puppydog is always a joy to live with, but an untrained and uncivilized dog can be a perpetual nightmare. Moreover, deny the dog an education and she will not have the opportunity to fulfill her own canine potential; neither will she have the ability to communicate effectively with her human companions.

Luckily, modern psychological training methods are easy, efficient, effective and, above all, considerably dog-friendly and user-friendly.

Doggy education is as simple as it is enjoyable. But before you can have a good time play-training with your new dog, you have to learn what to do and how to do it. There is no bigger variable influencing the success of dog training than the *owner's* experience and expertise. *Before you embark on the dog's education, you must first educate yourself.*

Basic Training for Owners

Ideally, basic owner training should begin well *before* you select your dog. Find out all you can about your chosen breed first, then master rudimentary training and handling skills. If you already have your puppydog, owner training is a dire emergency—the clock is ticking! Especially for puppies, the first few weeks at home are the most important and influential days in the dog's life. Indeed, the cause of most adolescent and adult problems may be traced back to the initial days the pup explores her new home. This is the time to establish the *status quo*—to teach the puppydog how you would like her to behave and so prevent otherwise quite predictable problems.

In addition to consulting breeders and breed books such as this one (which understandably have a positive breed bias), seek out as many pet owners with your breed as you can find. Good points are obvious. What you want to find out are the breed-specific *problems,* so you can nip them in the bud. In particular, you should talk to owners with *adolescent* dogs and make a list of all anticipated problems. Most important, *test drive* at least half a dozen adolescent and adult dogs of your breed yourself. An 8-week-old puppy is deceptively easy to handle, but she will acquire adult size, speed and strength in just four months, so you should learn now what to prepare for.

Puppy and pet dog training classes offer a convenient venue to locate pet owners and observe dogs in action. For a list of suitable trainers in your area, contact the Association of Pet Dog Trainers (see chapter 13). You may also begin your basic owner training by observing

other owners in class. Watch as many classes and test drive as many dogs as possible. Select an upbeat, dog-friendly, people-friendly, fun-and-games, puppydog pet training class to learn the ropes. Also, watch training videos and read training books. You must find out what to do and how to do it *before* you have to do it.

Principles of Training

Most people think training comprises teaching the dog to do things such as sit, speak and roll over, but even a 4-week-old pup knows how to do these things already. Instead, the first step in training involves teaching the dog human words for each dog behavior and activity and for each aspect of the dog's environment. That way you, the owner, can more easily participate in the dog's domestic education by directing her to perform specific actions appropriately, that is, at the right time, in the right place and so on. Training opens communication channels, enabling an educated dog to at least understand her owner's requests.

In addition to teaching a dog *what* we want her to do, it is also necessary to teach her *why* she should do what we ask. Indeed, 95 percent of training revolves around motivating the dog *to want to do* what we want. Dogs often understand what their owners want; they just don't see the point of doing it—especially when the owner's repetitively boring and seemingly senseless instructions are totally at odds with much more pressing and exciting doggy distractions. It is not so much the dog that is being stubborn or dominant; rather, it is the owner who has failed to acknowledge the dog's needs and feelings and to approach training from the dog's point of view.

The Meaning of Instructions

The secret to successful training is learning how to use training lures to predict or prompt specific behaviors—to coax the dog to do what you want *when* you want. Any highly valued object (such as a treat or toy) may be used as a lure, which the dog will follow with her eyes and nose. Moving the lure in specific ways entices the dog to move her nose, head and entire body in specific ways. In fact, by learning the art of manipulating various lures, it is possible to teach the dog to assume virtually any body position and perform any action. Once you have control over the expression of the dog's behaviors and can elicit any body position or behavior at will, you can easily teach the dog to perform on request.

Teach your dog words for each activity she needs to know, like down.

Tell your dog what you want her to do, use a lure to entice her to respond correctly, then profusely praise and maybe reward her once she performs the desired action. For example, verbally request "Tina, sit!" while you move a squeaky toy upwards and backwards over the dog's muzzle (lure-movement and hand signal), smile knowingly as she looks up (to follow the lure) and sits down (as a result of canine anatomical engineering), then praise her to distraction ("Gooood Tina!"). Squeak the toy, offer a training treat and give your dog and yourself a pat on the back.

Being able to elicit desired responses over and over enables the owner to reward the dog over and over. Consequently, the dog begins to think training is fun. For example, the more the dog is rewarded for sitting, the more she enjoys sitting. Eventually the dog comes to realize that, whereas most sitting is appreciated, sitting immediately upon request usually prompts especially enthusiastic praise and a slew of high-level rewards. The dog begins to sit on cue much of the time, showing that she is starting to grasp the meaning of the owner's verbal request and hand signal.

Why Comply?

Most dogs enjoy initial lure-reward training and are only too happy to comply with their owners' wishes. Unfortunately, repetitive drilling without appreciative feedback tends to diminish the dog's enthusiasm until she eventually fails to see the point of complying anymore. Moreover, as the dog approaches adolescence she becomes more easily distracted as she develops other interests. Lengthy sessions with repetitive exercises tend to bore and demotivate both parties. If it's not fun, the owner doesn't do it and neither does the dog.

Integrate training into your dog's life: The greater number of training sessions each day and the *shorter* they are, the more willingly compliant your dog will become. Make sure to have a short (just a few seconds) training interlude before every enjoyable canine activity. For example, ask your dog to sit to greet people, to sit before you throw her Frisbee and to sit for her supper. Really, sitting is no different from a canine "Please."

To train your dog, you need gentle hands, a loving heart and a good attitude.

Also, include numerous short training interludes during every enjoyable canine pastime, for example, when playing with the dog or when she is running in the park. In this fashion, doggy distractions may be effectively converted into rewards for training. Just as all games have rules, fun becomes training . . . and training becomes fun.

Eventually, rewards actually become unnecessary to continue motivating your dog. If trained with consideration and kindness, performing the desired behaviors will become self-rewarding and, in a sense, your dog will motivate herself. Just as it is not necessary to reward a human companion during an enjoyable walk in the park, or following a game of tennis, it is hardly necessary to reward our best friend—the dog—for walking by our side or while playing fetch. Human company during enjoyable activities is reward enough for most dogs.

Even though your dog has become self-motivating, it's still good to praise and pet her a lot and offer rewards once in a while, especially for a good job well done. And if for no other reason, praising and rewarding others is good for the human heart.

Punishment

Without a doubt, lure-reward training is by far the best way to teach: Entice your dog to do what you want and then reward her for doing so. Unfortunately, a human shortcoming is to take the good for granted and to moan and groan at the bad. Specifically, the dog's many good behaviors are ignored while the owner focuses on punishing the dog for making mistakes. In extreme cases, instruction is *limited* to punishing mistakes made by a trainee dog, child, employee or husband, even though it has been proven punishment training is notoriously inefficient and ineffective and is decidedly unfriendly and combative. It teaches the dog that training is a drag, almost as quickly as it teaches the dog to dislike her trainer. Why treat our best friends like our worst enemies?

Punishment training is also much more laborious and time consuming. Whereas it takes only a finite amount of time to teach a dog what to chew, for example, it takes much, much longer to punish the dog for each and every mistake. Remember, *there is only one right way!* So why not teach that right way from the outset?!

To make matters worse, punishment training causes severe lapses in the dog's reliability. Since it is obviously impossible to punish the dog each and every time she misbehaves, the dog quickly learns to distinguish between those times when she must comply (so as to avoid impending punishment) and those times when she need not comply, because punishment is impossible. Such times include when the dog is off leash and 6 feet away, when the owner is otherwise engaged (talking to a friend, watching television, taking a shower, tending to the baby or chatting on the telephone) or when the dog is left at home alone.

Instances of misbehavior will be numerous when the owner is away, because even when the dog complied in the owner's looming presence, she did so unwillingly. The dog was forced to act against her will, rather than molding her will to want to please. Hence, when the owner is absent, not only does the dog know she need not comply, she simply does not want to. Again, the trainee is not a stubborn vindictive beast, but rather the trainer has failed to teach. Punishment training invariably creates unpredictable Jekyll and Hyde behavior.

Trainer's Tools

Many training books extol the virtues of a vast array of training paraphernalia and electronic and metallic gizmos, most of which are designed for canine restraint, correction and punishment, rather than for actual facilitation of doggy education. In reality, most effective training tools are not found in stores; they come from within ourselves. In addition to a willing dog, all you really need is a functional human brain, gentle hands, a loving heart and a good attitude.

In terms of equipment, all dogs do require a quality buckle collar to sport dog tags and to attach the leash (for safety and to comply with local leash laws). Hollow chew toys (like Kongs or sterilized longbones) and a dog bed or collapsible crate are musts for housetraining. Three additional tools are required:

1. specific lures (training treats and toys) to predict and prompt specific desired behaviors;
2. rewards (praise, affection, training treats and toys) to reinforce for the dog what a lot of fun it all is; and
3. knowledge—how to convert the dog's favorite activities and games (potential distractions to training) into "life-rewards," which may be employed to facilitate training.

The most powerful of these is *knowledge.* Education is the key! Watch training classes, participate in training classes, watch videos, read books, enjoy play-training with your dog and then your dog will say "Please," and your dog will say "Thank you!"

Housetraining

If dogs were left to their own devices, certainly they would chew, dig and bark for entertainment and then no doubt highlight a few areas of their living space with sprinkles of urine, in much the same way we decorate by hanging pictures. Consequently, when we ask a dog to live with us, we must teach her *where* she may dig, *where* she may perform her toilet duties, *what* she may chew and *when* she may bark. After all, when left at home alone for many hours, we cannot expect the dog to amuse herself by completing crosswords or watching the soaps on TV!

Also, it would be decidedly unfair to keep the house rules a secret from the dog, and then get angry and punish the poor critter for inevitably transgressing rules she did not even know existed. Remember: Without adequate education and guidance, the dog will be forced to establish her own rules—doggy rules—and most probably will be at odds with the owner's view of domestic living.

Since most problems develop during the first few days the dog is at home, prospective dog owners must be certain they are quite clear about the principles of housetraining *before* they get a dog. Early misbehaviors quickly become established as the *status quo*—

becoming firmly entrenched as hard-to-break bad habits, which set the precedent for years to come. Make sure to teach your dog good habits right from the start. Good habits are just as hard to break as bad ones!

Ideally, when a new dog comes home, try to arrange for someone to be present as much as possible during the first few days (for adult dogs) or weeks for puppies. With only a little forethought, it is surprisingly easy to find a puppy sitter, such as a retired person, who would be willing to eat from your refrigerator and watch your television while keeping an eye on the newcomer to encourage the dog to play with chew toys and to ensure she goes outside on a regular basis.

Potty Training

To teach the dog where to relieve herself:

1. never let her make a single mistake;
2. let her know where you want her to go; and
3. handsomely reward her for doing so: "GOOOOOOOD DOG!!!" liver treat, liver treat, liver treat!

Preventing Mistakes

A single mistake is a training disaster, since it heralds many more in future weeks. And each time the dog soils the house, this further reinforces the dog's unfortunate preference for an indoor, carpeted toilet. *Do not let an unhousetrained dog have full run of the house.*

When you are away from home, or cannot pay full attention, confine the dog to an area where elimination is appropriate, such as an outdoor run or, better still, a small, comfortable indoor kennel with access to an outdoor run. When confined in this manner, most dogs will naturally housetrain themselves.

If that's not possible, confine the dog to an area, such as a utility room, kitchen, basement or garage, where elimination may not be desired in the long run but as an interim measure it is certainly preferable to doing it all around the house. Use newspaper to cover the floor of the dog's day room. The newspaper may be used to soak up the urine and to wrap up and dispose of the feces. Once your dog develops a preferred spot for eliminating, it is only necessary to cover that part of the floor with newspaper. The smaller papered area may then be moved (only a little each day) towards the door to the outside. Thus the dog will develop the tendency to go to the door when she needs to relieve herself.

The first few weeks at home are the most important and influential in your dog's life.

Never confine an unhousetrained dog to a crate for long periods. Doing so would force the dog to soil the crate and ruin its usefulness as an aid for housetraining (see the following discussion).

Teaching Where

In order to teach your dog where you would like her to do her business, you have to be there to direct the proceedings—an obvious, yet often neglected, fact of life. In order to be there to teach the dog *where* to go, you need to know *when* she needs to go. Indeed, the success of housetraining depends on the owner's ability to predict these times. Certainly, a regular feeding schedule will facilitate prediction somewhat, but there is nothing like "loading the deck" and influencing the timing of the outcome yourself!

Whenever you are at home, make sure the dog is under constant supervision and/or confined to a small

area. If already well trained, simply instruct the dog to lie down in her bed or basket. Alternatively, confine the dog to a crate (doggy den) or tie-down (a short, 18-inch lead that can be clipped to an eye hook in the baseboard near her bed). Short-term close confinement strongly inhibits urination and defecation, since the dog does not want to soil her sleeping area. Thus, when you release the puppydog each hour, she will definitely need to urinate immediately and defecate every third or fourth hour. Keep the dog confined to her doggy den and take her to her intended toilet area each hour, every hour and on the hour.

When taking your dog outside, instruct her to sit quietly before opening the door—she will soon learn to sit by the door when she needs to go out!

Teaching Why

Being able to predict when the dog needs to go enables the owner to be on the spot to praise and reward the dog. Each hour, hurry the dog to the intended toilet area in the yard, issue the appropriate instruction ("Go pee!" or "Go poop!"), then give the dog three to four minutes to produce. Praise and offer a couple of training treats when successful. The treats are important because many people fail to praise their dogs with feeling . . . and housetraining is hardly the time for understatement. So either loosen up and enthusiastically praise that dog: "Wuzzzer-wuzzer-wuzzer, hoooser good wuffer den? Hoooo went pee for Daddy?" Or say "Good dog!" as best you can and offer the treats for effect.

Following elimination is an ideal time for a spot of play-training in the yard or house. Also, an empty dog may be allowed greater freedom around the house for the next half hour or so, just as long as you keep an eye out to make sure she does not get into other kinds of mischief. If you are preoccupied and cannot pay full attention, confine the dog to her doggy den once more to enjoy a peaceful snooze or to play with her many chew toys.

If your dog does not eliminate within the allotted time outside—no biggie! Back to her doggy den, and then try again after another hour.

As I own large dogs, I always feel more relaxed walking an empty dog, knowing that I will not need to finish our stroll weighted down with bags of feces!

Beware of falling into the trap of walking the dog to get her to eliminate. The good ol' dog walk is such an enormous highlight in the dog's life that it represents the single biggest potential reward in domestic dogdom. However, when in a hurry, or during inclement weather, many owners abruptly terminate the walk the moment the dog has done her business. This, in effect, severely punishes the dog for doing the right thing, in the right place at the right time. Consequently, many dogs become strongly inhibited from eliminating outdoors because they know it will signal an abrupt end to an otherwise thoroughly enjoyable walk.

Instead, instruct the dog to relieve herself in the yard prior to going for a walk. If you follow the above instructions, most dogs soon learn to eliminate on cue. As soon as the dog eliminates, praise (and offer a treat or two)—"Good dog! Let's go walkies!" Use the walk as a reward for eliminating in the yard. If the dog does not go, put her back in her doggy den and think about a walk later on. You will find with a "No feces—no walk" policy, your dog will become one of the fastest defecators in the business.

If you do not have a backyard, instruct the dog to eliminate right outside your front door prior to the walk. Not only will this facilitate clean up and disposal of the feces in your own trash can but, also, the walk may again be used as a colossal reward.

Chewing and Barking

Short-term close confinement also teaches the dog that occasional quiet moments are a reality of domestic living. Your puppydog is extremely impressionable during her first few weeks at home. Regular

confinement at this time soon exerts a calming influence over the dog's personality. Remember, once the dog is housetrained and calmer, there will be a whole lifetime ahead for the dog to enjoy full run of the house and garden. On the other hand, by letting the newcomer have unrestricted access to the entire household and allowing her to run willy-nilly, she will most certainly develop a bunch of behavior problems in short order, no doubt necessitating confinement later in life. It would not be fair to remedially restrain and confine a dog you have trained, through neglect, to run free.

When confining the dog, make sure she always has an impressive array of suitable chew toys. Kongs and sterilized longbones (both readily available from pet stores) make the best chew toys, since they are hollow and may be stuffed with treats to heighten the dog's interest. For example, by stuffing the little hole at the top of a Kong with a small piece of freeze-dried liver, the dog will not want to leave it alone.

Remember, treats do not have to be junk food and they certainly should not represent extra calories. Rather, treats should be part of each dog's regular daily diet: Some food may be served in the dog's bowl for breakfast and dinner, some food may be used as training treats, and some food may be used for stuffing chew toys. I regularly stuff my dogs' many Kongs with different shaped biscuits and kibble. The kibble seems to fall out fairly easily, as do the oval-shaped biscuits, thus rewarding the dog instantaneously for checking out the chew toys. The bone-shaped biscuits fall out after a while, rewarding the dog for worrying at the chew toy. But the triangular biscuits never come out. They remain inside the Kong as lures,

Make sure your puppy has suitable chew toys.

maintaining the dog's fascination with her chew toy. To further focus the dog's interest, I always make sure to flavor the triangular biscuits by rubbing them with a little cheese or freeze-dried liver.

To teach come, call your dog, open your arms as a welcoming signal, wave a toy or a treat and praise for every step in your direction.

If stuffed chew toys are reserved especially for times the dog is confined, the puppydog will soon learn to enjoy quiet moments in her doggy den and she will quickly develop a chew-toy habit—a good habit! This is a simple *autoshaping* process; all the owner has to do is set up the situation and the dog all but trains herself—easy and effective. Even when the dog is given run of the house, her first inclination will be to indulge her rewarding chew-toy habit rather than destroy less-attractive household articles, such as curtains, carpets, chairs and compact disks. Similarly, a chew-toy chewer will be less inclined to scratch and chew herself excessively. Also, if the dog busies herself as a recreational chewer, she will be less inclined to develop into a recreational barker or digger when left at home alone.

Stuff a number of chew toys whenever the dog is left confined and remove the extra-special-tasting treats when you return. Your dog will now amuse herself with her chew toys before falling asleep and then resume playing with her chew toys when she expects you to return. Since most owner-absent misbehavior happens right after you leave and right before your expected return, your puppydog will now be conveniently preoccupied with her chew toys at these times.

Come and Sit

Most puppies will happily approach virtually anyone, whether called or not; that is, until they collide with adolescence and

develop other more important doggy interests, such as sniffing a multiplicity of exquisite odors on the grass. Your mission, Mr./Ms. Owner, is to teach and reward the pup for coming reliably, willingly and happily when called—and you have just three months to get it done. Unless adequately reinforced, your puppy's tendency to approach people will self-destruct by adolescence.

Call your dog ("Tina, come!"), open your arms (and maybe squat down) as a welcoming signal, waggle a treat or toy as a lure and reward the puppydog when she comes running. Do not wait to praise the dog until she reaches you—she may come 95 percent of the way and then run off after some distraction. Instead, praise the dog's *first* step towards you and continue praising enthusiastically for *every* step she takes in your direction.

When the rapidly approaching puppy dog is three lengths away from impact, instruct her to sit ("Tina, sit!") and hold the lure in front of you in an outstretched hand to prevent her from hitting you midchest and knocking you flat on your back! As Tina decelerates to nose the lure, move the treat upwards and backwards just over her muzzle with an upwards motion of your extended arm (palm-upwards). As the dog looks up to follow the lure, she will sit down (if she jumps up, you are holding the lure too high). Praise the dog for sitting. Move backwards and call her again. Repeat this many times over, always praising when Tina comes and sits; on occasion, reward her.

For the first couple of trials, use a training treat both as a lure to entice the dog to come and sit and as a reward for doing so. Thereafter, try to use different items as lures and rewards. For example, lure the dog with a Kong or Frisbee but reward her with a food treat. Or lure the dog with a food treat but pat her and throw a tennis ball as a reward. After just a few repetitions, dispense with the lures and rewards; the dog will begin to respond willingly to your verbal requests and hand signals just for the prospect of praise from your heart and affection from your hands.

Instruct every family member, friend and visitor how to get the dog to come and sit. Invite people over for a series of pooch parties; do not keep the pup a secret—let other people enjoy this puppy, and let the pup enjoy other people. Puppydog parties are not only fun, they easily attract a lot of people to help *you* train *your* dog. Unless you teach your dog how to meet people, that is, to sit for greetings, no doubt the dog will resort to jumping up. Then you and the visitors will get annoyed, and the dog will be punished. This is not fair. *Send out those invitations for puppy parties and teach your dog to be mannerly and socially acceptable.*

Even though your dog quickly masters obedient recalls in the house, her reliability may falter when playing in the backyard or local park. Ironically, it is *the owner* who has unintentionally trained the dog *not* to respond in these instances. By allowing the dog to play and run around and otherwise have a good time, but then to call the dog to put her on leash to take her home, the dog quickly learns playing is fun but training is a drag. Thus, playing in the park becomes a severe distraction, which works against training. Bad news!

Instead, whether playing with the dog off leash or on leash, request her to come at frequent intervals—say, every minute or so. On most occasions, praise and pet the dog for a few seconds while she is sitting, then tell her to go play again. For especially fast recalls, offer a couple of training treats and take the time to praise and pet the dog enthusiastically before releasing her. The dog will learn that coming when called is not necessarily the end of the play session, and neither is it the end of the world; rather, it signals an enjoyable, quality time-out with the owner before resuming play once more. In fact, playing in the park now becomes a very effective life-reward, which works to facilitate training by reinforcing each obedient and timely recall. Good news!

Sit, Down, Stand and Rollover

Teaching the dog a variety of body positions is easy for owner and dog, impressive for spectators and

extremely useful for all. Using lure-reward techniques, it is possible to train several positions at once to verbal commands or hand signals (which impress the socks off onlookers).

Sit and ***down***—the two control commands—prevent or resolve nearly a hundred behavior problems. For example, if the dog happily and obediently sits or lies down when requested, she cannot jump on visitors, dash out the front door, run around and chase her tail, pester other dogs, harass cats or annoy family, friends or strangers. Additionally, "Sit" or "Down" are the best emergency commands for off-leash control.

It is easier to teach and maintain a reliable sit than maintain a reliable recall. *Sit* is the purest and simplest of commands—either the dog is sitting or she is not. If there is any change of circumstances or potential danger in the park, for example, simply instruct the dog to sit. If she sits, you have a number of options: Allow the dog to resume playing when she is safe, walk up and put the dog on leash or call the dog. The dog will be much more likely to come when called if she has already acknowledged her compliance by sitting. If the dog does not sit in the park—train her to!

Stand and ***rollover-stay*** are the two positions for examining the dog. Your veterinarian will love you to distraction if you take a little time to teach the dog to stand still and roll over and play possum. Also, your vet bills will be smaller because it will take the veterinarian less time to examine your dog. The rollover-stay is an especially useful command and is really just a variation of the down-stay: Whereas the dog lies prone in the traditional down, she lies supine in the rollover-stay.

As with teaching come and sit, the training techniques to teach the dog to assume all other body positions on cue are user-friendly and dog-friendly. Simply give the appropriate request, lure the dog into the desired body position using a training treat or toy and then *praise* (and maybe reward) the dog as soon as she complies. Try not to touch the dog to get her to respond. If you teach the dog by guiding her into position, the dog will quickly learn that rump-pressure means sit, for example, but as yet you still have no control over your dog if she is just 6 feet away. It will still be necessary to teach the dog to sit on request. So do not make training a time-consuming two-step process; instead, teach the dog to sit to a verbal request or hand signal from the outset. Once the dog sits willingly when requested, by all means use your hands to pet the dog when she does so.

To teach ***down*** when the dog is already sitting, say "Tina, down!," hold the lure in one hand (palm down) and lower that hand to the floor between the dog's forepaws. As the dog lowers her head to follow the lure, slowly move the lure away from the dog just a fraction (in front of her paws). The dog will lie down as she stretches her nose forward to follow the lure. Praise the dog when she does so. If the dog stands up, you pulled the lure away too far and too quickly.

When teaching the dog to lie down from the standing position, say "Down" and lower the lure to the floor as before. Once the dog has lowered her forequarters and assumed a play bow, gently and slowly move the lure *towards* the dog between her forelegs. Praise the dog as soon as her rear end plops down.

After just a couple of trials it will be possible to alternate sits and downs and have the dog energetically perform doggy push-ups. Praise the dog a lot, and after half a dozen or so push-ups reward the dog with a training treat or toy. You will notice the more energetically you move your arm—upwards (palm up) to get the dog to sit, and downwards (palm down) to get the dog to lie down—the more energetically the dog responds to your requests. Now try training the dog in silence and you will notice she has also learned to respond to hand signals. Yeah! Not too shabby for the first session.

To teach ***stand*** from the sitting position, say "Tina, stand," slowly move the lure half a dog-length away from the dog's nose, keeping it at nose level, and praise the dog as she stands to follow the lure. As soon

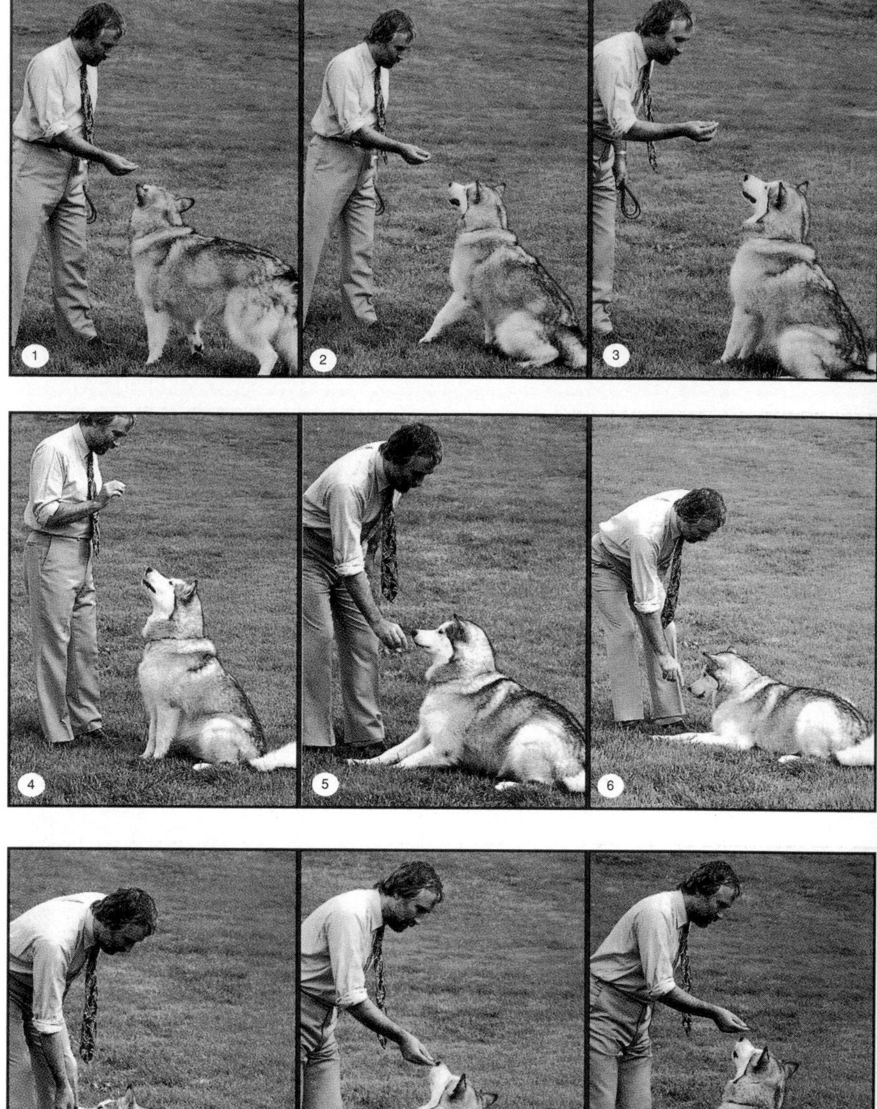

Using a food lure to teach sit, down and stand. 1) "Phoenix, sit." 2) Hand palm upwards, move lure up and back over dog's muzzle. 3) "Good sit, Phoenix!" 4) "Phoenix, down." 5) Hand palm downwards, move lure down to lie between dog's forepaws. 6) "Phoenix, off. Good down, Phoenix!" 7) "Phoenix, sit!" 8) Palm upwards, move lure up and back, keeping it close to dog's muzzle. 9) "Good sit, Phoenix!"

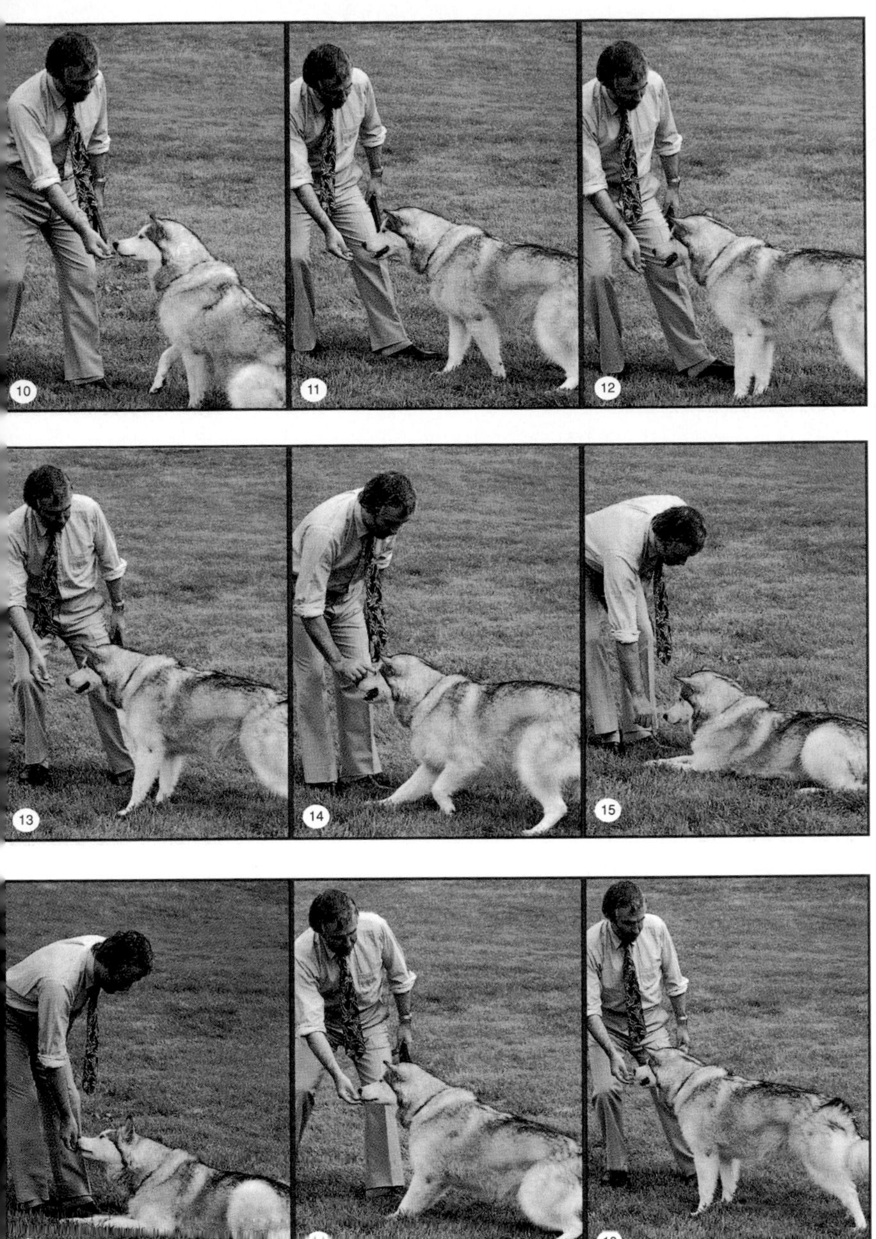

10) "Phoenix, stand!" 11) Move lure away from dog at nose height, then lower it a tad. 12) "Phoenix, off! Good stand, Phoenix!" 13) "Phoenix, down!" 14) Hand palm downwards, move lure down to lie between dog's forepaws. 15) "Phoenix, off! Good down-stay, Phoenix!" 16) "Phoenix, stand!" 17) Move lure away from dog's muzzle up to nose height. 18) "Phoenix, off! Good stand-stay, Phoenix. Now we'll make the vet and groomer happy!"

as the dog stands, lower the lure to just beneath the dog's chin to entice her to look down; otherwise she will stand and then sit immediately. To prompt the dog to stand from the down position, move the lure half a dog-length upwards and away from the dog, holding the lure at standing nose height from the floor.

Teaching ***rollover*** is best started from the down position, with the dog lying on one side, or at least with both hind legs stretched out on the same side. Say "Tina, bang!" and move the lure backwards and alongside the dog's muzzle to her elbow (on the side of her outstretched hind legs). Once the dog looks to the side and backwards, very slowly move the lure upwards to the dog's shoulder and backbone. Tickling the dog in the goolies (groin area) often invokes a reflex-raising of the hind leg as an appeasement gesture, which facilitates the tendency to roll over. If you move the lure too quickly and the dog jumps into the standing position, have patience and start again. As soon as the dog rolls onto her back, keep the lure stationary and mesmerize the dog with a relaxing tummy rub.

To teach ***rollover-stay*** when the dog is standing or moving, say "Tina, bang!" and give the appropriate hand signal (with index finger pointed and thumb cocked in true Sam Spade fashion), then in one fluid movement lure her to first lie down and then rollover-stay as above.

Teaching the dog to ***stay*** in each of the above four positions becomes a piece of cake after first teaching the dog not to worry at the toy or treat training lure. This is best accomplished by hand feeding dinner kibble. Hold a piece of kibble firmly in your hand and softly instruct "Off!" Ignore any licking and slobbering *for however long the dog worries at the treat,* but say "Take it!" and offer the kibble *the instant* the dog breaks contact with her muzzle. Repeat this a few times, and then up the ante and insist the dog remove her muzzle for one whole second before offering the kibble. Then progressively refine your criteria and have the dog not touch your hand (or treat) for longer and longer periods on each trial, such as for two seconds, four seconds, then six, ten, fifteen, twenty, thirty seconds and so on.

The dog soon learns: (1) worrying at the treat never gets results, whereas (2) noncontact is often rewarded after a variable time lapse.

Teaching ***"Off!"*** has many useful applications in its own right. Additionally, instructing the dog not to touch a training lure often produces spontaneous and magical stays. Request the dog to stand-stay, for example, and not to touch the lure. At first set your sights on a short two-second stay before rewarding the dog. (Remember, every long journey begins with a single step.) However, on subsequent trials, gradually and progressively increase the length of stay required to receive a reward. In no time at all your dog will stand calmly for a minute or so.

Relevancy Training

Once you have taught the dog what you expect her to do when requested to come, sit, lie down, stand, rollover and stay, the time is right to teach the dog *why* she should comply with your wishes. The secret is to have many (*many*) extremely short training interludes (two to five seconds each) at numerous (*numerous*) times during the course of the dog's day. Especially work with the dog immediately *before* the dog's good times and *during* the dog's good times. For example, ask your dog to sit and/or lie down each time before opening doors, serving meals, offering treats and tummy rubs; ask the dog to perform a few controlled doggy pushups before letting her off leash or throwing a tennis ball; and perhaps request the dog to sit-down-sit-stand-down-stand-rollover before inviting her to cuddle on the couch.

Similarly, request the dog to sit many times during play or on walks, and in no time at all the dog will be only too pleased to follow your instructions because she has learned that a compliant response heralds all sorts of goodies. Basically all you are trying to teach the dog is how to say please: "Please throw the tennis ball. Please may I snuggle on the couch."

Remember, it is important to keep training interludes short and to have many short sessions each and every day. The shortest (and most useful) session comprises asking the dog to sit and then go play during a play session. When trained this way, your dog will soon associate training with good times. In fact, the dog may be unable to distinguish between training and good times and, indeed, there should be no distinction. The warped concept that training involves forcing the dog to comply and/or dominating her will is totally at odds with the picture of a truly well-trained dog. In reality, enjoying a game of training with a dog is no different from enjoying a game of backgammon or tennis with a friend; and walking with a dog should be no different from strolling with a spouse, or with buddies on the golf course.

Walk by Your Side

Many people attempt to teach a dog to heel by putting her on a leash and physically correcting the dog when she makes mistakes. There are a number of things seriously wrong with this approach, the first being that most people do not want precision heeling; rather, they simply want the dog to follow or walk by their side. Second, when physically restrained during "training," even though the dog may grudgingly mope by your side when "handcuffed" on leash, let's see what happens when she is off leash. History! The dog is in the next county because she never enjoyed walking with you on leash and you have no control over her off leash. So let's just teach the dog off leash from the outset to *want* to walk with us. Third, if the dog has not been trained to heel, it is a trifle hasty to think about punishing the poor dog for making mistakes and breaking heeling rules she didn't even know existed. This is simply not fair! Surely, if the dog had been adequately taught how to heel, she would seldom make mistakes and hence there would be no need to correct the dog. Remember, each mistake and each correction (punishment) advertise the trainer's inadequacy, not the dog's. The dog is not stubborn, she is not stupid and she is not bad. Even if she were, she would still require training, so let's train her properly.

Let's teach the dog to *enjoy* following us and to *want* to walk by our side off leash. Then it will be easier to teach high-precision off-leash heeling patterns if desired. Before going on outdoor walks, it is necessary to teach the dog not to pull. Then it becomes easy to teach on-leash walking and heeling because the dog already wants to walk with you, she is familiar with the desired walking and heeling positions and she knows not to pull.

Following

Start by training your dog to follow you. Many puppies will follow if you simply walk away from them and maybe click your fingers or chuckle. Adult dogs may require additional enticement to stimulate them to follow, such as a training lure or, at the very least, a lively trainer. To teach the dog to follow: (1) keep walking and (2) walk away from the dog. If the dog attempts to lead or lag, change pace; slow down if the dog forges too far ahead, but speed up if she lags too far behind. Say "Steady!" or "Easy!" each time before you slow down and "Quickly!" or "Hustle!" each time before you speed up, and the dog will learn to change pace on cue. If the dog lags or leads too far, or if she wanders right or left, simply walk quickly in the opposite direction and maybe even run away from the dog and hide.

Practicing is a lot of fun; you can set up a course in your home, yard or park to do this. Indoors, entice the dog to follow upstairs, into a bedroom, into the bathroom, downstairs, around the living room couch, zigzagging between dining room chairs and into the kitchen for dinner. Outdoors, get the dog to follow around park benches, trees, shrubs and along walkways and lines in the grass. (For safety outdoors, it is advisable to attach a long line on the dog, but never exert corrective tension on the line.)

Remember, following has a lot to do with attitude—*your* attitude! Most probably your dog will *not* want to follow Mr. Grumpy Troll with the personality of wilted lettuce. Lighten up—walk with a jaunty step, whistle a happy tune, sing, skip and tell jokes to your dog and she will be right there by your side.

By Your Side

It is smart to train the dog to walk close on one side or the other—either side will do, your choice. When walking, jogging or cycling, it is generally bad news to have the dog suddenly cut in front of you. In fact, I train my dogs to walk "By my side" and "Other side"—both very useful instructions. It is possible to position the dog fairly accurately by looking to the appropriate side and clicking your fingers or slapping your thigh on that side. A precise positioning may be attained by holding a training lure, such as a chew toy, tennis ball or food treat. Stop and stand still several times throughout the walk, just as you would when window shopping or meeting a friend. Use the lure to make sure the dog slows down and stays close whenever you stop.

When teaching the dog to heel, we generally want her to sit in heel position when we stop. Teach heel

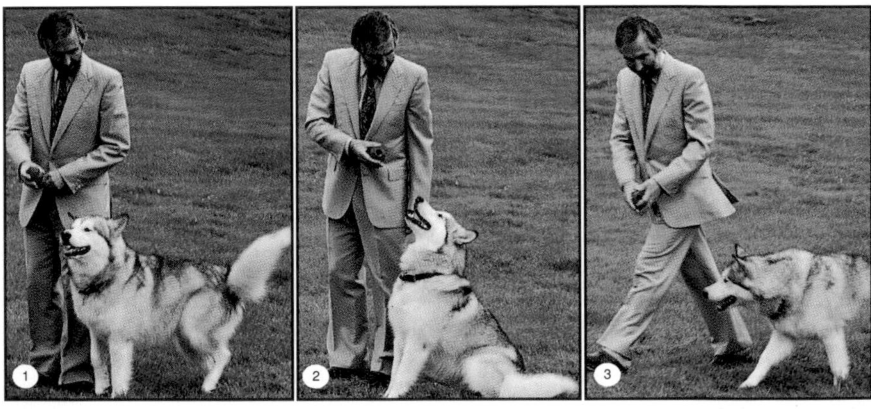

Using a toy to teach sit-heel-sit sequences: 1) "Phoenix, sit!" Standing still, move lure up and back over dog's muzzle . . . 2) to position dog sitting in heel position on your left side. 3) Say "Phoenix, heel!" and walk ahead, wagging lure in left hand. Change lure to right hand in preparation for sit signal. Say "Sit" and then . . .

position at the standstill and the dog will learn that the default heel position is sitting by your side (left or right—your choice, unless you wish to compete in obedience trials, in which case the dog must heel on the left).

Several times a day, stand up and call your dog to come and sit in heel position—"Tina, heel!" For example, instruct the dog to come to heel each time there are commercials on TV, or each time you turn a page of a novel, and the dog will get it in a single evening.

Practice straight-line heeling and turns separately. With the dog sitting at heel, teach her to turn in place. After each quarter-turn, half-turn or full turn in place, lure the dog to sit at heel. Now it's time for short straight-line heeling sequences, no more than a few steps at a time. Always think of heeling in terms of sit-heel-sit sequences—start and end with the dog in position and do your best to keep her there when moving. Progressively increase the number of steps in each sequence. When the dog remains close for 20 yards of straight-line heeling, it is time to add a few turns and then sign up for a happy-heeling obedience class to get some advice from the experts.

4) use hand signal to lure dog to sit as you stop. Eventually, dog will sit automatically at heel whenever you stop. 5) "Good dog!"

No Pulling on Leash

You can start teaching your dog not to pull on leash anywhere—in front of the television or outdoors—but regardless of location, you must not take a single step with tension in the leash. For a reason known only to dogs, even just a couple of paces of pulling on leash is intrinsically motivating and diabolically rewarding. Instead, attach the leash to the dog's collar, grasp the other end firmly with both hands held close to your chest, and stand still—do not budge an inch. Have somebody watch you with a stopwatch to time your progress, or else you will never believe this will work and so you will not even try the exercise, and your shoulder and the dog's neck will be traumatized for years to come.

Stand still and wait for the dog to stop pulling, and to sit and/or lie down. All dogs stop pulling and sit eventually. Most take only a couple of minutes; the all-time record is 22½ minutes. Time how long it takes. Gently praise the dog when she stops pulling, and as soon as she sits, enthusiastically praise the dog and take just one step forward, then immediately stand still. This single step usually demonstrates the ballistic reinforcing nature of pulling on leash; most dogs explode to the end of the leash, so be prepared for the strain. Stand firm and wait for the dog to sit again. Repeat this half a dozen times and you will probably notice a progressive reduction in the force of the dog's one-step explosions and a radical reduction in the time it takes for the dog to sit each time.

As the dog learns "Sit we go" and "Pull we stop," she will begin to walk forward calmly with each single step and automatically sit when you stop. Now try two steps before you stop. Wooooooo! Scary! When the dog has mastered two steps at a time, try for three. After each success, progressively increase the number of steps in the sequence: try four steps and then six, eight, ten and twenty steps before stopping. Congratulations! You are now walking the dog on leash.

Whenever walking with the dog (off leash or on leash), make sure you stop periodically to practice a few position commands and stays before instructing the dog to "Walk on!" (Remember, you want the dog to be compliant everywhere, not just in the kitchen when her dinner is at hand.) For example, stopping every 25 yards to briefly train the dog amounts to over 200 training interludes within a single 3-mile stroll. And each training session is in a different location. You will not believe the improvement within just the first mile of the first walk.

To put it another way, integrating training into a walk offers 200 separate opportunities to use the continuance of the walk as a reward to reinforce the dog's education. Moreover, some training interludes may comprise continuing education for the dog's walking skills: Alternate short periods of the dog walking calmly by your side with periods when the dog is allowed to sniff and investigate the environment. Now sniffing odors on the grass and meeting other dogs become rewards which reinforce the dog's calm and mannerly demeanor. Good Lord! Whatever next? Many enjoyable walks together of course. Happy trails!

THE IMPORTANCE OF TRICKS

Nothing will improve a dog's quality of life better than having a few tricks under her belt. Teaching any trick expands the dog's vocabulary, which facilitates communication and improves the owner's control. Also, specific tricks help prevent and resolve specific behavior problems. For example, by teaching the dog to fetch her toys, the dog learns carrying a toy makes the owner happy and, therefore, will be more likely to chew her toy than other inappropriate items.

More important, teaching tricks prompts owners to lighten up and train with a sunny disposition. Really, tricks should be no different from any other behaviors we put on cue. But they are. When teaching tricks, owners have a much sweeter attitude, which in turn motivates the dog and improves her willingness to comply. The dog feels tricks are a blast, but formal commands are a drag. In fact, tricks are so enjoyable, they may be used as rewards in training by asking the dog to come, sit and down-stay and then rollover for a tummy rub. Go on, try it: Crack a smile and even giggle when the dog promptly and willingly lies down and stays.

Most important, performing tricks prompts onlookers to smile and giggle. Many people are scared of dogs, especially large ones. And nothing can be more off-putting for a dog than to be constantly confronted by strangers who don't like her because of her size or the way she looks. Uneasy people put the dog on edge, causing her to back off and bark, only frightening people all the more. And so a vicious circle develops, with the people's fear fueling the dog's fear *and vice versa*. Instead, tie a pink ribbon to your dog's collar and practice all sorts of tricks on walks and in the park, and you will be pleasantly amazed how it changes people's attitudes toward your friendly dog. The dog's repertoire of tricks is limited only by the trainer's imagination. Below I have described three of my favorites:

SPEAK AND SHUSH

The training sequence involved in teaching a dog to bark on request is no different from that used when training any behavior on cue: request—lure—response—reward. As always, the secret of success lies in finding an effective lure. If the dog always barks at the doorbell, for example, say "Rover, speak!", have an accomplice ring the doorbell, then reward the dog for barking. After a few woofs, ask Rover to "Shush!", waggle a food treat under her nose (to entice her to sniff and thus to shush), praise her when quiet and eventually offer the treat as a reward. Alternate "Speak" and "Shush," progressively increasing the length of shush-time between each barking bout.

PLAY BOW

With the dog standing, say "Bow!" and lower the food lure (palm upwards) to rest between the dog's forepaws. Praise as the dog lowers her forequarters and sternum to the ground (as when teaching the down), but then lure the dog to stand and offer the treat. On successive trials, gradually increase the length of time the dog is required to remain in the play bow posture in order to gain a food reward. If the dog's rear end collapses into a down, say nothing and offer no reward; simply start over.

BE A BEAR

With the dog sitting backed into a corner to prevent her from toppling over backwards, say "Be a bear!" With bent paw and palm down, raise a lure upwards and backwards along the top of the dog's muzzle. Praise the dog when she sits up on her haunches and offer the treat as a reward. To prevent the dog from standing on her hind legs, keep the lure closer to the dog's muzzle. On each trial, progressively increase the length of time the dog is required to sit up to receive a food reward. Since lure-reward training is so easy, teach the dog to stand and walk on her hind legs as well!

Teaching "Be a Bear"

chapter 9

Getting Active with your Dog

by Bardi McLennan

Once you and your dog have graduated from basic obedience training and are beginning to work together as a team, you can take part in the growing world of dog activities. There are so many fun things to do with your dog! Just remember, people and dogs don't always learn at the same pace, so don't be upset if you (or your dog) need more than two basic training courses before your team becomes operational. Even smart dogs don't go straight to college from kindergarten!

Just as there are events geared to certain types of dogs, so there are ones that are more appealing to certain types of people. In some activities, you give the commands and your dog does the work (upland game hunting is one example), while in others, such as agility, you'll both get a workout. You may want to aim for prestigious titles to add to your dog's name, or you may want nothing more than the sheer enjoyment of being around other people and their dogs. Passive or active, participation has its own rewards.

All dogs seem to love playing flyball.

Consider your dog's physical capabilities when looking into any of the canine activities. It's easy to see that a Basset Hound is not built for the racetrack, nor would a Chihuahua be the breed of choice for pulling a sled. A loyal dog will attempt almost anything you ask him to do, so it is up to you to know your dog's limitations. A dog must be physically sound in order to compete at any level in athletic activities, and being mentally sound is a definite plus. Advanced age, however, may not be a deterrent. Many dogs still hunt and herd at ten or twelve years of age. It's entirely possible for dogs to be "fit at 50." Take your dog for a checkup, explain to your vet the type of activity you have in mind and be guided by his or her findings.

You needn't be restricted to breed-specific sports if it's only fun you're after. Certain AKC activities are limited to designated breeds; however, as each new trial, test or sport has grown in popularity, so has the variety of breeds encouraged to participate at a fun level.

But don't shortchange your fun, or that of your dog, by thinking only of the basic function of her breed. Once a dog has learned how to learn, she can be taught to do just about anything as long as the size of the dog is right for the job and you both think it is fun and rewarding. In other words, you are a team.

To get involved in any of the activities detailed in this chapter, look for the names and addresses of the organizations that sponsor them in Chapter 13. You can also ask your breeder or a local dog trainer for contacts.

You can compete in obedience trials with a well trained dog.

Official American Kennel Club Activities

The following tests and trials are some of the events sanctioned by the AKC and sponsored by various dog clubs. Your dog's expertise will be rewarded with impressive titles. You can participate just for fun, or be competitive and go for those awards.

Obedience

Training classes begin with pups as young as three months of age in kindergarten puppy training, then advance to pre-novice (all exercises on lead) and go on to novice, which is where you'll start off-lead work. In obedience classes dogs learn to sit, stay, heel and come through a variety of exercises. Once you've got the basics down, you can enter obedience trials and work toward earning your dog's first degree, a C.D. (Companion Dog).

The next level is called "Open," in which jumps and retrieves perk up the dog's interest. Passing grades in competition at this level earn a C.D.X. (Companion Dog Excellent). Beyond that lies the goal of the most ambitious—Utility (U.D. and even U.D.X. or OTCh, an Obedience Champion).

Agility

All dogs can participate in the latest canine sport to have gained worldwide popularity for its fun and excitement, agility. It began in England as a canine version of horse show-jumping, but because dogs are more agile and able to perform on verbal commands, extra feats were added such as climbing, balancing and racing through tunnels or in and out of weave poles. Many of the obstacles (regulation or homemade) can be set up in your own backyard. If the agility bug bites, you could end up in international competition!

For starters, your dog should be obedience trained, even though, in the beginning, the lessons may all be taught on lead. Once the dog understands the commands (and you do, too), it's as easy as guiding the dog over a prescribed course, one obstacle at a time. In competition, the race is against the clock, so wear your running shoes! The dog starts with 200 points and the judge deducts for infractions and misadventures along the way.

All dogs seem to love agility and respond to it as if they were being turned loose in a playground paradise. Your dog's enthusiasm will be contagious; agility turns into great fun for dog and owner.

TITLES AWARDED BY THE AKC

Conformation: Ch. (Champion)

Obedience: CD (Companion Dog); CDX (Companion Dog Excellent); UD (Utility Dog); UDX (Utility Dog Excellent); OTCh. (Obedience Trial Champion)

Field: JH (Junior Hunter); SH (Senior Hunter); MH (Master Hunter); AFCh. (Amateur Field Champion); FCh. (Field Champion)

Lure Coursing: JC (Junior Courser); SC (Senior Courser)

Herding: HT (Herding Tested); PT (Pre-Trial Tested); HS (Herding Started); HI (Herding Intermediate); HX (Herding Excellent); HCh. (Herding Champion)

Tracking: TD (Tracking Dog); TDX (Tracking Dog Excellent)

Agility: NAD (Novice Agility); OAD (Open Agility); ADX (Agility Excellent); MAX (Master Agility)

Earthdog Tests: JE (Junior Earthdog); SE (Senior Earthdog); ME (Master Earthdog)

Canine Good Citizen: CGC

Combination: DC (Dual Champion—Ch. and Fch.), TC (Triple Champion—Ch., Fch., and OTCh.)

Field Trials and Hunting Tests

There are field trials and hunting tests for the sporting breeds—retrievers, spaniels and pointing breeds, and for some hounds—Bassets, Beagles and Dachshunds. Field trials are competitive events that test a dog's ability to perform the functions for which she was bred. Hunting tests, which are open to retrievers,

spaniels and pointing breeds only, are noncompetitive and are a means of judging the dog's ability as well as that of the handler.

Hunting is a very large and complex part of canine sports, and if you own one of the breeds that hunts, the events are a great treat for your dog and you. He gets to do what he was bred for, and you get to work with him and watch him do it. You'll be proud of and amazed at what your dog can do.

Fortunately, the AKC publishes a series of booklets on these events, which outline the rules and regulations and include a glossary of the sometimes complicated terms. The AKC also publishes newsletters for field trialers and hunting test enthusiasts. The United Kennel Club (UKC) also has informative materials for the hunter and his dog.

Retrievers and other sporting breeds get to do what they're bred to in hunting tests.

Herding Tests and Trials

Herding, like hunting, dates back to the first known uses man made of dogs. The interest in herding today is widespread, and if you own a herding breed, you can join in the activity. Herding dogs are tested for their natural skills to keep a flock of ducks, sheep or cattle together. If your dog shows potential, you can start at the testing level, where your dog can earn a title for showing an inherent herding ability. With training you can advance to the trial level, where your dog should be capable of controlling even difficult livestock in diverse situations.

Lure Coursing

The AKC Tests and Trials for Lure Coursing are open to traditional sighthounds—Greyhounds, Whippets,

Borzoi, Salukis, Afghan Hounds, Ibizan Hounds and Scottish Deerhounds—as well as to Basenjis and Rhodesian Ridgebacks. Hounds are judged on overall ability, follow, speed, agility and endurance. This is possibly the most exciting of the trials for spectators, because the speed and agility of the dogs is awesome to watch as they chase the lure (or "course") in heats of two or three dogs at a time.

Tracking

Tracking is another activity in which almost any dog can compete because every dog that sniffs the ground when taken outdoors is, in fact, tracking. The hard part comes when the rules as to what, when and where the dog tracks are determined by a person, not the dog! Tracking tests cover a large area of fields, woods and roads. The tracks are laid hours before the dogs go to work on them, and include "tricks" like cross-tracks and sharp turns. If you're interested in search-and-rescue work, this is the place to start.

This tracking dog is hot on the trail.

Earthdog Tests for Small Terriers and Dachshunds

These tests are open to Australian, Bedlington, Border, Cairn, Dandie Dinmont, Smooth and Wire Fox, Lakeland, Norfolk, Norwich, Scottish, Sealyham, Skye, Welsh and West Highland White Terriers as well as Dachshunds. The dogs need no prior training for this terrier sport. There is a qualifying test on the day of the event, so dog and handler learn the rules on the spot. These tests, or "digs," sometimes end with informal races in the late afternoon.

Here are some of the extracurricular obedience and racing activities that are not regulated by the AKC or UKC, but are generally run by clubs or a group of dog fanciers and are often open to all.

Canine Freestyle This activity is something new on the scene and is variously likened to dancing, dressage or ice skating. It is meant to show the athleticism of the dog, but also requires showmanship on the part of the dog's handler. If you and your dog like to ham it up for friends, you might want to look into freestyle.

Lure coursing lets sighthounds do what they do best—run!

Scent Hurdle Racing Scent hurdle racing is purely a fun activity sponsored by obedience clubs with members forming competing teams. The height of the hurdles is based on the size of the shortest dog on the team. On a signal, one team dog is released on each of two side-by-side courses and must clear every hurdle before picking up its own dumbbell from a platform and returning over the jumps to the handler. As each dog returns, the next on that team is sent. Of course, that is what the dogs are supposed to do. When the dogs improvise (going under or around the hurdles, stealing another dog's dumbbell, and so forth), it no doubt frustrates the handlers, but just adds to the fun for everyone else.

Flyball This type of racing is similar, but after negotiating the four hurdles, the dog comes to a flyball box, steps on a lever that releases a tennis ball into the air, catches the ball and returns over the hurdles to the starting point. This game also becomes extremely fun for spectators because the dogs sometimes cheat by catching a ball released by the dog in the next lane. Three titles can be earned—Flyball Dog (F.D.), Flyball Dog Excellent (F.D.X.) and Flyball Dog Champion (Fb.D.Ch.)—all awarded by the North American Flyball Association, Inc.

Dogsledding The name conjures up the Rocky Mountains or the frigid North, but you can find dogsled clubs in such unlikely spots as Maryland, North Carolina and Virginia! Dogsledding is primarily for the Nordic breeds such as the Alaskan Malamutes, Siberian Huskies and Samoyeds, but other breeds can try. There are some practical backyard applications to this sport, too. With parental supervision, almost any strong dog could pull a child's sled.

Coming over the A-frame on an agility course.

These are just some of the many recreational ways you can get to know and understand your multifaceted dog better and have fun doing it.

chapter 10

Your Dog and your Family

by Bardi McLennan

Adding a dog automatically increases your family by one, no matter whether you live alone in an apartment or are part of a mother, father and six kids household. The single-person family is fair game for numerous and varied canine misconceptions as to who is dog and who pays the bills, whereas a dog in a houseful of children will consider himself to be just one of the gang, littermates all. One dog and one child may give a dog reason to believe they are both kids or both dogs. Either interpretation requires parental supervision and sometimes speedy intervention.

As soon as one paw goes through the door into your home, Rufus (or Rufina) has to make many adjustments to become a part of your family. Your job is to make him fit in as painlessly as possible. An older dog may have some frame of reference from past experience, but to a 10-week-old puppy, everything is brand new: people, furniture, stairs, when and where people eat, sleep or watch TV, his own place and everyone else's space, smells, sounds, outdoors—everything!

Puppies, and newly acquired dogs of any age, do not need what we think of as "freedom." If you leave a new dog or puppy loose in the house, you will almost certainly return to chaotic destruction and the dog will forever after equate your homecoming with a time of punishment to be dreaded. It is unfair to give your dog what amounts to "freedom to get into trouble." Instead, confine him to a crate for brief periods of your absence (up to three or four hours) and, for the long haul, a workday for example, confine him to one untrashable area with his own toys, a bowl of water and a radio left on (low) in another room.

Lots of pets get along with each other just fine.

For the first few days, when not confined, put Rufus on a long leash tied to your wrist or waist. This umbilical cord method enables the dog to learn all about you from your body language and voice, and to learn by his own actions which things in the house are NO! and which ones are rewarded by "Good dog." House-training will be easier with the pup always by your side. Speaking of which, accidents do happen. That goal of "completely housetrained" takes up to a year, or the length of time it takes the pup to mature.

The All-Adult Family

Most dogs in an adults-only household today are likely to be latchkey pets, with no one home all day but the

dog. When you return after a tough day on the job, the dog can and should be your relaxation therapy. But going home can instead be a daily frustration.

Separation anxiety is a very common problem for the dog in a working household. It may begin with whines and barks of loneliness, but it will soon escalate into a frenzied destruction derby. That is why it is so important to set aside the time to teach a dog to relax when left alone in his confined area and to understand that he can trust you to return.

Let the dog get used to your work schedule in easy stages. Confine him to one room and go in and out of that room over and over again. Be casual about it. No physical, voice or eye contact. When the pup no longer even notices your comings and goings, leave the house for varying lengths of time, returning to stay home for a few minutes and gradually increasing the time away. This training can take days, but the dog is learning that you haven't left him forever and that he can trust you.

Any time you leave the dog, but especially during this training period, be casual about your departure. No anxiety-building fond farewells. Just "Bye" and go! Remember the "Good dog" when you return to find everything more or less as you left it.

If things are a mess (or even a disaster) when you return, greet the dog, take him outside to eliminate, and then put him in his crate while you clean up. Rant and rave in the shower! *Do not* punish the dog. You were not there when it happened, and the rule is: Only punish as you catch the dog in the act of wrongdoing. Obviously, it makes sense to get your latchkey puppy when you'll have a week or two to spend on these training essentials.

Family weekend activities should include Rufus whenever possible. Depending on the pup's age, now is the time for a long walk in the park, playtime in the backyard, a hike in the woods. Socializing is as important as health care, good food and physical exercise, so visiting Aunt Emma or Uncle Harry and the next-door neighbor's dog or cat is essential to developing an outgoing, friendly temperament in your pet.

If you are a single adult, socializing Rufus at home and away will prevent him from becoming overly protective of you (or just overly attached) and will also prevent such behavioral problems as dominance or fear of strangers.

Babies

Whether already here or on the way, babies figure larger than life in the eyes of a dog. If the dog is there first, let him in on all your baby preparations in the house. When baby arrives, let Rufus sniff any item of clothing that has been on the baby before Junior comes home. Then let Mom greet the dog first before introducing the new family member. Hold the baby down for the dog to see and sniff, but make sure someone's holding the dog on lead in case of any sudden moves. Don't play keep-away or tease the dog with the baby, which only invites undesirable jumping up.

Dogs are perfect confidants.

The dog and the baby are "family," and for starters can be treated almost as equals. Things rapidly change, however, especially when baby takes to creeping around on all fours on the dog's turf or, better yet, has yummy pudding all over her face and hands! That's when a lot of things in the dog's and baby's lives become more separate than equal.

Toddlers make terrible dog owners, but if you can't avoid the combination, use patient discipline (that is, positive teaching rather than punishment), and use time-outs before you run out of patience.

A dog and a baby (or toddler, or an assertive young child) should never be left alone together. Take the dog with you or confine him. With a baby or youngsters in the house, you'll have plenty of use for that wonderful canine safety device called a crate!

Young Children

Any dog in a house with kids will behave pretty much as the kids do, good or bad. But even good dogs and good children can get into trouble when play becomes rowdy and active.

Teach children how to play nicely with a puppy.

Legs bobbing up and down, shrill voices screeching, a ball hurtling overhead, all add up to exuberant frustration for a dog who's just trying to be part of the gang. In a pack of puppies, any legs or toys being chased would be caught by a set of teeth, and all the pups involved would understand that is how the game is played. Kids do not understand this, nor do parents tolerate it. Bring Rufus indoors before you have reason to regret it. This is time-out, not a punishment.

You can explain the situation to the children and tell them they must play quieter games until the puppy learns not to grab them with his mouth. Unfortunately, you can't explain it that easily to the dog. With adult supervision, they will learn how to play together.

Young children love to tease. Sticking their faces or wiggling their hands or fingers in the dog's face is teasing. To another person it might be just annoying, but it is threatening to a dog. There's another difference: We can make the child stop by an explanation, but the only way a dog can stop it is with a warning growl and then with teeth. Teasing is the major cause of children being bitten by their pets. Treat it seriously.

Older Children

The best age for a child to get a first dog is between the ages of 8 and 12. That's when kids are able to accept some real responsibility for their pet. Even so, take the child's vow of "I will never *ever* forget to feed (brush, walk, etc.) the dog" for what it's worth: a child's good intention at that moment. Most kids today have extra lessons, soccer practice, Little League, ballet, and so forth piled on top of school schedules. There will be many times when Mom will have to come to the dog's rescue. "I walked the dog for you so you can set the table for me" is one way to get around a missed appointment without laying on blame or guilt.

Kids in this age group make excellent obedience trainers because they are into the teaching/learning process themselves and they lack the self-consciousness of adults. Attending a dog show is something the whole family can enjoy, and watching Junior Showmanship may catch the eye of the kids. Older children can begin to get involved in many of the recreational activities that were reviewed in the previous chapter. Some of the agility obstacles, for example, can be set up in the backyard as a family project (with an adult making sure all the equipment is safe and secure for the dog).

Older kids are also beginning to look to the future, and may envision themselves as veterinarians or trainers or show dog handlers or writers of the next Lassie best-seller. Dogs are perfect confidants for these dreams. They won't tell a soul.

Other Pets

Introduce all pets tactfully. In a dog/cat situation, hold the dog, not the cat. Let two dogs meet on neutral turf—a stroll in the park or a walk down the street—with both on loose leads to permit all the normal canine ways of saying hello, including routine sniffing, circling, more sniffing, and so on. Small creatures such as hamsters, chinchillas or mice must be kept safe from their natural predators (dogs and cats).

Festive Family Occasions

Parties are great for people, but not necessarily for puppies. Until all the guests have arrived, put the dog in his crate or in a room where he won't be disturbed. A socialized dog can join the fun later as long as he's not underfoot, annoying guests or into the hors d'oeuvres.

There are a few dangers to consider, too. Doors opening and closing can allow a puppy to slip out unnoticed in the confusion, and you'll be organizing a search party instead of playing host or hostess. Party food and buffet service are not for dogs. Let Rufus party in his crate with a nice big dog biscuit.

At Christmas time, not only are tree decorations dangerous and breakable (and perhaps family heirlooms), but extreme caution should be taken with the lights, cords and outlets for the tree lights and any other festive lighting. Occasionally a dog lifts a leg, ignoring the fact that the tree is indoors. To avoid this, use a canine repellent, made for gardens, on the tree. Or keep him out of the tree room unless supervised. And whatever you do, *don't* invite trouble by hanging his toys on the tree!

Car Travel

Before you plan a vacation by car or RV with Rufus, be sure he enjoys car travel. Nothing spoils a holiday quicker than a carsick dog! Work within the dog's comfort level. Get in the car with the dog in his crate or attached to a canine car safety belt and just sit there until he relaxes. That's all. Next time, get in the car, turn on the engine and go nowhere. Just sit. When that is okay, turn on the engine and go around the block. Now you can go for a ride and include a stop where you get out, leaving the dog for a minute or two.

On a warm day, always park in the shade and leave windows open several inches. And return quickly. It only takes 10 minutes for a car to become an overheated steel death trap.

Motel or Pet Motel?

Not all motels or hotels accept pets, but you have a much better choice today than even a few years ago. To find a dog-friendly lodging, look at *On the Road Again With Man's Best Friend*, a series of directories that detail bed and breakfasts, inns, family resorts and other hotels/motels. Some places require a refundable deposit to cover any damage incurred by the dog. More B&Bs accept pets now, but some restrict the size.

If taking Rufus with you is not feasible, check out boarding kennels in your area. Your veterinarian may offer this service, or recommend a kennel or two he or she is familiar with. Go see the facilities for yourself, ask about exercise, diet, housing, and so on. Or, if you'd rather have Rufus stay home, look into bonded petsitters, many of whom will also bring in the mail and water your plants.

chapter 11

Your Dog and your Community

by Bardi McLennan

Step outside your home with your dog and you are no longer just family, you are both part of your community. This is when the phrase "responsible pet ownership" takes on serious implications. For starters, it means you pick up after your dog—not just occasionally, but every time your dog eliminates away from home. That means you have joined the Plastic Baggy Brigade! You always have plastic sandwich bags in your pocket and several in the car. It means you teach your kids how to use them, too. If you think this is "yucky," just imagine what the person (a non-doggy person) who inadvertently steps in the mess thinks!

Your responsibility extends to your neighbors: To their ears (no annoying barking); to their property (their garbage, their lawn, their flower beds, their cat—especially their cat); to their kids (on bikes, at play); to their kids' toys and sports equipment.

There are numerous dog-related laws, ranging from simple dog licensing and leash laws to those holding you liable for any physical injury or property damage done by your dog. These laws are in place to protect everyone in the community, including you and your dog. There are town ordinances and state laws which are by no means the same in all towns or all states. Ignorance of the law won't get you off the hook. The time to find out what the laws are where you live is now.

Dressing your dog up makes him appealing to strangers.

Be sure your dog's license is current. This is not just a good local ordinance, it can make the difference between finding your lost dog or not. Many states now require proof of rabies vaccination and that the dog has been spayed or neutered before issuing a license. At the same time, keep up the dog's annual immunizations.

Never let your dog run loose in the neighborhood. This will not only keep you on the right side of the leash law, it's the outdoor version of the rule about not giving your dog "freedom to get into trouble."

Good Canine Citizen

Sometimes it's hard for a dog's owner to assess whether or not the dog is sufficiently socialized to be accepted by the community at large. Does Rufus or Rufina display good, controlled behavior in public? The AKC's Canine Good Citizen program is available through many dog organizations. If your dog passes the test, the title "CGC" is earned.

The overall purpose is to turn your dog into a good neighbor and to teach you about your responsibility to your community as a dog owner. Here are the ten things your dog must do willingly:

1. Accept a stranger stopping to chat with you.
2. Sit and be petted by a stranger.
3. Allow a stranger to handle him or her as a groomer or veterinarian would.
4. Walk nicely on a loose lead.
5. Walk calmly through a crowd.
6. Sit and down on command, then stay in a sit or down position while you walk away.
7. Come when called.
8. Casually greet another dog.
9. React confidently to distractions.
10. Accept being left alone with someone other than you and not become overly agitated or nervous.

Schools and Dogs

Schools are getting involved with pet ownership on an educational level. It has been proven that children who are kind to animals are humane in their attitude toward other people as adults.

A dog is a child's best friend, and so children are often primary pet owners, if not the primary caregivers. Unfortunately, they are also the ones most often bitten by dogs. This occurs due to a lack of understanding that pets, no matter how sweet, cuddly and loving, are still animals. Schools, along with parents, dog clubs, dog fanciers and the AKC, are working to change all that with video programs for children not only in grade school, but in the nursery school and pre-kindergarten age group. Teaching youngsters how to be responsible dog owners is important community work. When your dog has a CGC, volunteer to take part in an educational classroom event put on by your dog club.

Boy Scout Merit Badge

A Merit Badge for Dog Care can be earned by any Boy Scout ages 11 to 18. The requirements are not easy, but amount to a complete course in responsible dog care and general ownership. Here are just a few of the things a Scout must do to earn that badge:

Point out ten parts of the dog using the correct names.

Give a report (signed by parent or guardian) on your care of the dog (feeding, food used, housing, exercising, grooming and bathing), plus what has been done to keep the dog healthy.

Explain the right way to obedience train a dog, and demonstrate three comments.

Several of the requirements have to do with health care, including first aid, handling a hurt dog, and the dangers of home treatment for a serious ailment.

The final requirement is to know the local laws and ordinances involving dogs.

There are similar programs for Girl Scouts and 4-H members.

Local Clubs

Local dog clubs are no longer in existence just to put on a yearly dog show. Today, they are apt to be the hub of the community's involvement with pets. Dog clubs conduct educational forums with big-name speakers, stage demonstrations of canine talent in a busy mall and take dogs of various breeds to schools for classroom discussion.

The quickest way to feel accepted as a member in a club is to volunteer your services! Offer to help with something—anything—and watch your popularity (and your interest) grow.

Therapy Dogs

Once your dog has earned that essential CGC and reliably demonstrates a steady, calm temperament, you could look into what therapy dogs are doing in your area.

Therapy dogs go with their owners to visit patients at hospitals or nursing homes, generally remaining on leash but able to coax a pat from a stiffened hand, a smile from a blank face, a few words from sealed lips or a hug from someone in need of love.

Your dog can make a difference in lots of lives.

Nursing homes cover a wide range of patient care. Some specialize in care of the elderly, some in the treatment of specific illnesses, some in physical therapy. Children's facilities also welcome visits from trained therapy dogs for boosting morale in their pediatric patients. Hospice care for the terminally ill and the at-home care of AIDS patients are other areas where this canine visiting is desperately needed. Therapy dog training comes first.

There is a lot more involved than just taking your nice friendly pooch to someone's bedside. Doing therapy dog work involves your own emotional stability as well as that of your dog. But once you have met all the requirements for this work, making the rounds once a week or once a month with your therapy dog is possibly the most rewarding of all community activities.

Disaster Aid

This community service is definitely not for everyone, partly because it is time-consuming. The initial training is rigorous, and there can be no let-up in the continuing workouts, because members are on call 24 hours a day to go wherever they are needed at a moment's notice. But if you think you would like to be able to assist in a disaster, look into search-and-rescue work. The network of search-and-rescue volunteers is worldwide, and all members of the American Rescue Dog Association (ARDA) who are qualified to do this work are volunteers who train and maintain their own dogs.

Physical Aid

Making the rounds with your therapy dog can be very rewarding.

Most people are familiar with Seeing Eye dogs, which serve as blind people's eyes, but not with all the other work that dogs are trained to do to assist the disabled. Dogs are also specially trained to pull wheelchairs, carry school books, pick up dropped objects, open and close doors. Some also are ears for the deaf. All these assistance-trained dogs, by the way, are allowed anywhere "No Pet" signs exist (as are therapy dogs when properly identified). Getting started in any of this fascinating work requires a background in dog training and canine behavior, but there are also volunteer jobs ranging from answering the phone to cleaning out kennels to providing a foster home for a puppy. You have only to ask.

part four

Beyond the Basics

chapter 12

Recommended Reading

Books

About Health Care

Ackerman, Lowell. *Guide to Skin and Haircoat Problems in Dogs.* Loveland, Colo.: Alpine Publications, 1994.

Alderton, David. *The Dog Care Manual.* Hauppauge, N.Y.: Barron's Educational Series, Inc., 1986.

American Kennel Club. *American Kennel Club Dog Care and Training.* New York: Howell Book House, 1991.

Bamberger, Michelle, DVM. *Help! The Quick Guide to First Aid for Your Dog.* New York: Howell Book House, 1995.

Carlson, Delbert, DVM, and James Giffin, MD. *Dog Owner's Home Veterinary Handbook.* New York: Howell Book House, 1992.

DeBitetto, James, DVM, and Sarah Hodgson. *You & Your Puppy.* New York: Howell Book House, 1995.

Humphries, Jim, DVM. *Dr. Jim's Animal Clinic for Dogs.* New York: Howell Book House, 1994.

McGinnis, Terri. *The Well Dog Book.* New York: Random House, 1991.

Pitcairn, Richard and Susan. *Natural Health for Dogs.* Emmaus, Pa.: Rodale Press, 1982.

About Dog Shows

Hall, Lynn. *Dog Showing for Beginners.* New York: Howell Book House, 1994.

Nichols, Virginia Tuck. *How to Show Your Own Dog.* Neptune, N. J.: TFH, 1970.

Vanacore, Connie. *Dog Showing, An Owner's Guide.* New York: Howell Book House, 1990.

About Training

Ammen, Amy. *Training in No Time.* New York: Howell Book House, 1995.

Baer, Ted. *Communicating With Your Dog.* Hauppauge, N.Y.: Barron's Educational Series, Inc., 1989.

Benjamin, Carol Lea. *Dog Problems.* New York: Howell Book House, 1989.

Benjamin, Carol Lea. *Dog Training for Kids.* New York: Howell Book House, 1988.

Benjamin, Carol Lea. *Mother Knows Best.* New York: Howell Book House, 1985.

Benjamin, Carol Lea. *Surviving Your Dog's Adolescence.* New York: Howell Book House, 1993.

Bohnenkamp, Gwen. *Manners for the Modern Dog.* San Francisco: Perfect Paws, 1990.

Dibra, Bashkim. *Dog Training by Bash.* New York: Dell, 1992.

Dunbar, Ian, PhD, MRCVS. *Dr. Dunbar's Good Little Dog Book,* James & Kenneth Publishers, 2140 Shattuck Ave. #2406, Berkeley, Calif. 94704. (510) 658–8588. Order from the publisher.

Dunbar, Ian, PhD, MRCVS. *How to Teach a New Dog Old Tricks,* James & Kenneth Publishers. Order from the publisher; address above.

Dunbar, Ian, PhD, MRCVS, and Gwen Bohnenkamp. Booklets on *Preventing Aggression; Housetraining; Chewing; Digging; Barking; Socialization; Fearfulness; and Fighting,* James & Kenneth Publishers. Order from the publisher; address above.

Evans, Job Michael. *People, Pooches and Problems.* New York: Howell Book House, 1991.

Kilcommons, Brian and Sarah Wilson. *Good Owners, Great Dogs.* New York: Warner Books, 1992.

McMains, Joel M. *Dog Logic—Companion Obedience.* New York: Howell Book House, 1992.

Rutherford, Clarice and David H. Neil, MRCVS. *How to Raise a Puppy You Can Live With.* Loveland, Colo.: Alpine Publications, 1982.

Volhard, Jack and Melissa Bartlett. *What All Good Dogs Should Know: The Sensible Way to Train.* New York: Howell Book House, 1991.

About Breeding

Harris, Beth J. Finder. *Breeding a Litter, The Complete Book of Prenatal and Postnatal Care.* New York: Howell Book House, 1983.

Holst, Phyllis, DVM. *Canine Reproduction.* Loveland, Colo.: Alpine Publications, 1985.

Walkowicz, Chris and Bonnie Wilcox, DVM. *Successful Dog Breeding, The Complete Handbook of Canine Midwifery.* New York: Howell Book House, 1994.

About Activities

American Rescue Dog Association. *Search and Rescue Dogs.* New York: Howell Book House, 1991.

Barwig, Susan and Stewart Hilliard. *Schutzhund.* New York: Howell Book House, 1991.

Beaman, Arthur S. *Lure Coursing.* New York: Howell Book House, 1994.

Daniels, Julie. *Enjoying Dog Agility—From Backyard to Competition.* New York: Doral Publishing, 1990.

Davis, Kathy Diamond. *Therapy Dogs.* New York: Howell Book House, 1992.

Gallup, Davis Anne. *Running With Man's Best Friend.* Loveland, Colo.: Alpine Publications, 1986.

Habgood, Dawn and Robert. *On the Road Again With Man's Best Friend.* New England, Mid-Atlantic, West Coast and Southeast editions. Selective guides to area bed and breakfasts, inns, hotels and resorts that welcome guests and their dogs. New York: Howell Book House, 1995.

Holland, Vergil S. *Herding Dogs.* New York: Howell Book House, 1994.

LaBelle, Charlene G. *Backpacking With Your Dog.* Loveland, Colo.: Alpine Publications, 1993.

Simmons-Moake, Jane. *Agility Training, The Fun Sport for All Dogs.* New York: Howell Book House, 1991.

Spencer, James B. *Hup! Training Flushing Spaniels the American Way.* New York: Howell Book House, 1992.

Spencer, James B. *Point! Training the All-Seasons Birddog.* New York: Howell Book House, 1995.

Tarrant, Bill. *Training the Hunting Retriever.* New York: Howell Book House, 1991.

Volhard, Jack and Wendy. *The Canine Good Citizen.* New York: Howell Book House, 1994.

General Titles

Haggerty, Captain Arthur J. *How to Get Your Pet Into Show Business.* New York: Howell Book House, 1994.

McLennan, Bardi. *Dogs and Kids, Parenting Tips.* New York: Howell Book House, 1993.

Moran, Patti J. *Pet Sitting for Profit, A Complete Manual for Professional Success.* New York: Howell Book House, 1992.

Scalisi, Danny and Libby Moses. *When Rover Just Won't Do, Over 2,000 Suggestions for Naming Your Dog.* New York: Howell Book House, 1993.

Sife, Wallace, PhD. *The Loss of a Pet.* New York: Howell Book House, 1993.

Wrede, Barbara J. *Civilizing Your Puppy.* Hauppauge, N.Y.: Barron's Educational Series, 1992.

Magazines

The AKC GAZETTE, The Official Journal for the Sport of Purebred Dogs. American Kennel Club, 51 Madison Ave., New York, NY.

Bloodlines Journal. United Kennel Club, 100 E. Kilgore Rd., Kalamazoo, MI.

Dog Fancy. Fancy Publications, 3 Burroughs, Irvine, CA 92718

Dog World. Maclean Hunter Publishing Corp., 29 N. Wacker Dr., Chicago, IL 60606.

Videos

"SIRIUS Puppy Training," by Ian Dunbar, PhD, MRCVS. James & Kenneth Publishers, 2140 Shattuck Ave. #2406, Berkeley, CA 94704. Order from the publisher.

"Training the Companion Dog," from Dr. Dunbar's British TV Series, James & Kenneth Publishers. (See address above).

The American Kennel Club produces videos on every breed of dog, as well as on hunting tests, field trials and other areas of interest to purebred dog owners. For more information, write to AKC/Video Fulfillment, 5580 Centerview Dr., Suite 200, Raleigh, NC 27606.

chapter 13

Resources

Breed Clubs

Every breed recognized by the American Kennel Club has a national (parent) club. National clubs are a great source of information on your breed. You can get the name of the secretary of the club by contacting:

The American Kennel Club
51 Madison Avenue
New York, NY 10010
(212) 696-8200

There are also numerous all-breed, individual breed, obedience, hunting and other special-interest dog clubs across the country. The American Kennel Club can provide you with a geographical list of clubs to find ones in your area. Contact them at the above address.

Registry Organizations

Registry organizations register purebred dogs. The American Kennel Club is the oldest and largest in this country, and currently recognizes over 130 breeds. The United Kennel Club registers some breeds the AKC doesn't (including the American Pit Bull Terrier and the Miniature Fox Terrier) as well as many of the same breeds. The others included here are for your reference; the AKC can provide you with a list of foreign registries.

American Kennel Club
51 Madison Avenue
New York, NY 10010

United Kennel Club (UKC)
100 E. Kilgore Road
Kalamazoo, MI 49001-5598

American Dog Breeders Assn.
P.O. Box 1771
Salt Lake City, UT 84110
(Registers American Pit Bull Terriers)

Canadian Kennel Club
89 Skyway Avenue
Etobicoke, Ontario
Canada M9W 6R4

National Stock Dog Registry
P.O. Box 402
Butler, IN 46721
(Registers working stock dogs)

Orthopedic Foundation for Animals (OFA)
2300 E. Nifong Blvd.
Columbia, MO 65201-3856
(Hip registry)

Activity Clubs

Write to these organizations for information on the activities they sponsor.

American Kennel Club
51 Madison Avenue
New York, NY 10010
(Conformation Shows, Obedience Trials, Field Trials and Hunting Tests, Agility, Canine Good

Citizen, Lure Coursing, Herding, Tracking, Earthdog Tests, Coonhunting.)

United Kennel Club
100 E. Kilgore Road
Kalamazoo, MI 49001-5598
(Conformation Shows, Obedience Trials, Agility, Hunting for Various Breeds, Terrier Trials and more.)

North American Flyball Assn.
1342 Jeff St.
Ypsilanti, MI 48198

International Sled Dog Racing Assn.
P.O. Box 446
Norman, ID 83848-0446

North American Working Dog Assn., Inc.
Southeast Kreisgruppe
P.O. Box 833
Brunswick, GA 31521

Trainers

Association of Pet Dog Trainers
P.O. Box 385
Davis, CA 95617
(800) PET–DOGS

American Dog Trainers' Network
161 West 4th St.
New York, NY 10014
(212) 727–7257

National Association of Dog Obedience Instructors
2286 East Steel Rd.
St. Johns, MI 48879

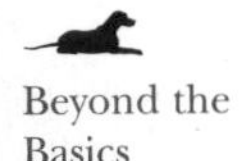

Associations

American Dog Owners Assn.
1654 Columbia Tpk.
Castleton, NY 12033
(Combats anti-dog legislation)

Delta Society
P.O. Box 1080
Renton, WA 98057-1080
(Promotes the human/animal bond through pet-assisted therapy and other programs)

Dog Writers Assn. of America (DWAA)
Sally Cooper, Secy.
222 Woodchuck Ln.
Harwinton, CT 06791

National Assn. for Search and Rescue (NASAR)
P.O. Box 3709
Fairfax, VA 22038

Therapy Dogs International
6 Hilltop Road
Mendham, NJ 07945